275

William Law on Christian Perfection

Edited and Abridged by Erwin Randolph

Bethany Fellowship INC.
MINNEAPOLIS, MINNESOTA 55438

Originally published under the title:
Christian Perfection

William Law on Christian Perfection
William Law

Library of Congress Catalog Card Number 80-70457

ISBN 0-87123-117-4

Copyright © 1975
Creation House
All Rights Reserved

Published by Bethany Fellowship, Inc.,
6820 Auto Club Road, Minneapolis, Minnesota 55438

Printed in the United States of America

Contents

Introduction

One may encounter those who through the years pay tribute to the thought and influence of William Law (1686-1761), but in recent times the accomplishments of this spiritual giant have been largely overlooked. One of the reasons for this neglect may be that some of his works were of a controversial sort relating primarily to issues of his day. Another reason may be that his later mystical works were somewhat misunderstood because they contained esoteric and speculative language. But much of what he wrote is too noteworthy for us to dismiss casually.

Many have fallen under Law's spell since Samuel Johnson's first encounter with *A Serious Call* . . . when he commended it as "the finest piece of hortatory theology in any language."[1] Although John Wesley did not always agree with Law, he maintained his respect for Law's extraordinary piety and spiritual counsel and was influenced by him to write his own *A Plain Account of Christian Perfection.*[2] Others who admired Law's thought include Leslie Stephen, Rufus Jones, Edward Gibbon and John H. Newman. Aldous Huxley thought Law was even more talented than Samuel Johnson, and wrote the following to Alan Watts in 1944:

> I have been reading William Law—with the greatest pleasure and profit. What a really wonderful writer, when he is at his best. It is sadly typical of our education that we are all made to read the second-rate amiabilities of Addison and Steele—but that one of the greatest masters of devotion and of philosophical theology is passed over almost in silence.[3]

1. James Boswell. *Life of Samuel Johnson (1794),* (London, 1893), p. 216.
2. See J. B. Green, *John Wesley and William Law* (London, 1945) and Eric C. Baker, *A Herald of the Evangelical Revival* (London, 1948).
3. Grover Smith, Ed., *The Letters of Aldous Huxley,* (Harper and Row, 1970) p. 504.

Even more recently, C. S. Lewis wrote in a letter of Law's devotional admonitions, ". . . about prides, superiorities, and affronts, there's no better book . . . . [There] you'll find all of us pierced like butterflies on cards."

* * * * *

In a way, to read any part of the biography of William Law is to encounter the devotional strain which impregnated his entire life and thought. As one writer put it, "His life of purity and self-denial is of one piece with his devotional writings."[4] Few men have exemplified more completely how to desire nothing in this world but to do the will of God.

Born in 1686 at King's Cliffe, near Stanford, Northamptonshire, England, William Law (the fourth of eight sons in a family of eleven children), came from a background "of high respectability and of good means."[5] Few details are known of his early years, but he entered Emmanuel College, Cambridge, as Sizar in 1705, which evidenced an early plan to enter the ministry of the Church of England.[6] He must have shown considerable promise as a student, for as far as we know he was the only one of the children whom his father sent to the University. He received the B.A. degree in 1708, a Fellowship to Emmanuel College in 1711 (the same year in which he was ordained) and the M.A. degree in 1712. While at the University, according to Byrom, Law's personal friend and biographer, he gave diligent attention to the reading of the classics, philosophy, Hebrew and French. He probably became familiar with numerous writings of the Church Fathers, a few of the fourteenth-century English mystics, and such devotional writers as St. Francis de Sales, Fenelon, and Thomas á Kempis.[7] He also wrote a thesis on Nicolas Malebranche.[8]

4. R. N. Flew, *The Idea of Perfection in Christian Theology* (London, 1934), p. 299.
5. J. H. Overton, *William Law, Nonjuror and Mystic* (London 1881), p. 5.
6. Law's appointment as Sizar meant that he was to receive from the University an allowance towards college expenses in exchange for "certain menial tasks." See Colin Wilson, "William Law" in *Religion and the Rebel* (New York, 1957), p. 209.
7. See Stephen Hobhouse, "William Law's Sources" in *Selected Mystical Writings of William Law* (London, 1948), pp. 361-367. Hobhouse here presents the likely sources for Law's ideas as based on the latter's own statements in his published works, parallels between his and other writings, statements of John Byrom in the *Journals*, and the more than six-hundred books left in the library at King's Cliffe, which Law presumably read.
8. Overton, *William Law, Nonjuror and Mystic*, p. 8.

There is no evidence that Law participated actively in the political controversies of the day. However, his refusal to take oaths of allegiance and abjuration upon the accession of George I exemplified his determination to put personal conviction above convenience—even though this decision meant his loss of Fellowship at Cambridge and permanent denial of the right to serve as a minister in the Church of England. His decision not to go on with the career for which he had prepared distressed him greatly. He wrote in a letter to his brother:

> My prospect indeed is melancholy enough, but had I done what was required of me to avoid it, I should have thought my condition much worse. The benefits of my education seem partly at an end, but that same education had been miserably lost if I had not learnt to fear something more than misfortune.[9]

The deprivation of a formal church assignment, however, did not embitter him. He continued to attend regularly his parish church and abstained from recriminatory remarks against churchmen who opposed his position as nonjuror.

A gap appears in Law's biography after he left the University, but we know that his father died in 1714, his mother in 1718, and that by 1723 he was back at Cambridge with young Edward Gibbon, the father of historian Edward Gibbon.[10] Thereafter Law appeared regularly in the Gibbon household at Putney as private tutor and chaplain.[11] Upon the death of the elder Gibbon in 1737, this relationship dissolved.

After a brief stay in London in 1738 and 1739, Law took up permanent residence at King's Cliffe, Northampton, where his manner of life continued to exemplify the high standard of piety

9. Christopher Walton, *Notes and Materials for an Adequate Biography of . . . William Law* (London, 1854), p. 344.

10. There is considerable conjecture about Law's activities after he left Cambridge. Most biographical accounts say that he went to London and officiated as Curate at St. Mary's Chruch in the Strand; however, Hobhouse cites evidence that Law held the Curacy at Haslingfield before he became a nonjuror. Hobhouse also holds to the 1723 date as marking the beginning of the Law-Gibbon association, although Overton and others prefer 1727. See *Selected Mystical Writings,* pp. 388-389.

11. Edward Gibbon, the historian, pays tribute to Law's intellect and scholarly manner.

recommended in his writings. He now personally supervised the school for orphan girls which he had founded in 1723; he distributed food and clothing to the poor of the community. He also served as spiritual adviser to two well-bred women: Miss Hester Gibbon, aunt of the historian, and Sarah Hutcheson, whose dying husband recommended that after his death she place herself under the spiritual direction of Law. Later this trio founded two almshouses and a school for boys.[12]

A few of the interesting particulars of Law's daily life at King's Cliffe were collected by C. Walton, Law's biographer:

> Mr. Law rose early each morning, probably about five o'clock, spending some time in devotion, after which he breakfasted, generally on a cup of chocolate in his bedroom, and then commenced to study . . . . Mr. Law kept four cows, the produce of which, beyond what was required for his household, he gave to the poor, distributing the milk every morning with his own hands . . . . At nine o'clock a bell was rung for family devotion, of which the Collects and Psalms for the day formed a portion. From . . . the performance of this duty Mr. Law retired in silence to his chamber, where he passed the morning in study, not infrequently interrupted by the message of some poor mendicant for aid, which never failed to secure his immediate attention . . . . Amongst the articles of clothing which he provided for the indigent were shirts made of strong coarse linen; and that he might not give away what he himself could not thankfully receive, he always wore them himself first . . . after which they were washed and distributed . . . .[13]

There exists no authentic portrait of Law, but Walton's description of his physical appearance and personal habits provides additional insight into the serious manner and righteous purpose which characterized his whole life:

> In stature, Mr. Law was rather over than under middle size; his frame was not corpulent, but stoutly built, and kept in healthy action by the unflinching discipline and regularity

---

12. Law not only gave freely of his own fortune to charity but also persuaded his companions at King's Cliffe to give of theirs. Mrs. Hutcheson's annual income was estimated at two to three thousand pounds, Miss Hester Gibbon's at about one thousand.

13. Walton, *Notes and Materials* . . . . p. 497 ff.

of his habits. The general form of his countenance was round; and he possessed a blunt felicitous readiness of utterance. He had well-proportioned features, which were recommended by a cheerful open expression, and probably became more decided as he advanced in years, the natural effect of his strong judgment and of the studious gravity of his youth. His face was ruddy; his eyes grey, clear, vivacious, sparkling with noble benignity, and with the keen wit which as his writings testify, was always ruled, like a well-broken but generous stud, by his superior wisdom. His general manner was lively and unaffected, and though his walk and conversation among his friends was that of a sage, we have the testimony . . . that he was accustomed to see company, and was a man of free conversation . . . Perhaps the gravity of his looks and demeanor was a little heightened by the soberness of his dress, which was usually a clerical hat, with the loops let down, black coat, and grey wig.[14]

Until the very end of his life Law manifested a pious spirit to those about him:

Mr. Law lived to the age of seventy-five without the infirmities of age . . . His eye was still piercing, for it was the organ of his immortal soul filled with Divine light. His heart was filled with God, and therefore his voice was the sweet trumpeter of Divine love.[15]

After catching a cold at the annual audit of the school accounts during Easter week in 1761, he developed a kidney inflammation, which resulted in his death in less than two weeks. According to Miss Gibbon, everything which he spoke during the affliction was of joy and divine transport, and he died singing a hymn.[16]

* * * * *

The attention which Law gave to his own devotional life at King's Cliffe was very singular. Alexander Whyte suggests that after his early religious controversies with Hoadley, Mandeville, and Tindal, he felt a need for a renewal of personal humility and devo-

---

14. Walton, *Notes and Materials* . . . , p. 502.
15. Overton, *William Law, Nonjuror and Mystic*, p. 444.
16. Overton, p. 446.

tion. Whyte notes also that Law collected a manuscript of choice forms of devotion, including confessions, petitions and praises from the Psalter, and arranged them topically for his own use. [17] He continually may have admonished others to improve their spiritual lives, but like Chaucer's Parson, he first practiced pious rule himself.

(Although scholars generally agree that Law's writings after 1735 were written under the effects of new mystical influences, not all of them agree as to the extent to which those influences caused him to alter his former beliefs. Whyte points up the "early" and "later" Law as contrasts in spiritual emphasis, while more recent studies by Hopkinson and others insist upon only slight alterations in his early tenets of faith.)

Written at approximately the same time in Law's career, both *Christian Perfection* (1726) and *A Serious Call* (1727) are similar in their recommendations for pious living. *A Serious Call* has been more readily available both in England and America, although *Christian Perfection* went through at least four editions in England before 1737. [18] The present edition marks the first appearance of *Christian Perfection* in this country that we know of.

Although the original title reads *A Practical Treatise Upon Christian Perfection,* the work is essentially devotional. Briefly defined, devotional literature is that substantial body of religious writing that has as its primary concern God's intimate dealings with the human heart. It centers upon several distinguishing themes: ways and means of achieving perfection; how to find acceptance with God; discerning the implications of worship; and approaching God intuitively. [19] It also emphasizes that beyond mere creed, one must possess the inner life of the Spirit and seek to emulate the example of Christ. Law, like such devotionalists as St. Augustine, Thomas á Kempis, Jeremy Taylor, and Lancelot Andrewes, has as his primary purpose the aiding of man in his quest for the godly life.

That *Christian Perfection* is essentially a book of devotion was

---

17. Alexander Whyte, *Characters and Characteristics,* (London, 1893) p. xxxi.
18. A.R. Walker, *William Law: His Life and Work* (S.P.C.K., 1973), p. 54.
19. Erwin Paul Rudolph, "A Study of the Religious Thought of William Law (1686-1761)," unpubl. Ph.D. diss. (University of Illinois, 1962), pp. 7-36.

recognized by many of Law's contemporaries. Speaking of this work, Bishop Wilson said, "Law's *Christian Perfection* fell into my hands by Providence, and after reading it I recommended it so heartily to a friend near London that he procured eighteen copies for each of our parochial libraries; I have recommended it to my clergy after the most affecting manner as the likeliest way to bring them to a most serious temper."[20] The prefatory advertisement to the 1893 edition states, "The *Christian Perfection* is the first work of Law's which as a beacon directs the wayfarer through the straight gate into the narrow way with its pitfalls and manifold difficulties which he knew so well and along which he himself had passed."[21]

The practical rules which Law lays down for achieving perfection are very close to the rules allegedly drawn up by himself when he was at Cambridge:

I. To fix deep in my mind that I have one business upon my hands—to seek for eternal happiness by doing the will of God.

II. To examine everything that relates to me in this view, as it serves or obstructs this only end of life.

III. To think nothing great or desirable because the world thinks it so; but to form all my judgments of things from the infallible Word of God, and direct my life according to it.

IV. To avoid all concerns with the world, or the ways of it, but where religion and charity oblige me to act.

V. To remember frequently, and impress it upon my mind deeply, that no condition of this life is for enjoyment, but for trial; and that every power, ability, or advantage we have are all so many talents to be accounted for to the Judge of all the world.

VI. That the greatness of human nature consists in doing nothing else but in imitating the Divine nature. That, therefore, all the greatness of this world, which is not in good actions, is perfectly beside the point.

VII. To remember often and seriously how much time is thrown away, from which I can expect nothing but the charge of guilt; and how little there may be to come on which an eternity depends.

20. Overton, *William Law, Nonjuror* . . . , pp. 48-49. This is a quotation from Bishop Wilson's letter to Lady Elizabeth Hastings, dated Warrington, September 13, 1729.
21. Law, *Works*, III pp. [iii]-iv.

VIII. To avoid all excess in eating and drinking.

IX. To spend as little time as I possibly can among such persons as can receive no benefit from me, nor I from them.

X. To be always fearful of letting my time slip away without some fruit.

XI. To avoid all idleness.

XII. To call to mind the presence of God whenever I find myself under temptation to sin and to have immediate recourse to prayer.

XIII. To think humbly of myself; and with great charity of all others.

XIV. To forbear from all evil speaking.

XV. To think often of the life of Christ, and to propose it as a pattern for myself.

XVI. To pray, privately, thrice a day, besides my morning and evening prayer.

XVII. To keep from _____ as much as I can without offence.[22]

XVIII. To spend some time in giving an account of the day previous to evening prayer: How have I spent this day? What sin have I committed? What temptations have I withstood? Have I performed all my duty?[23]

One may assume safely that Law's ideas on perfection were not completely original, for striving for perfection has long been emphasized by those who have incited others to pious living. François Fénelon, with whose works Law was evidently familiar, also wrote a well-known devotional book on Christian perfection which may have set Law to thinking about the subject. Fénelon, who was deeply moved by the possibility of achieving a state of perfection in this life, wrote letters of spiritual counsel and direction to persons living in the late seventeenth century. He dealt with several aspects of the spiritual life which are also handled by Law, such as the use of one's time, the imitation of Christ, how to know God, and self-renunciation.[24] Both men depict the same yearning for high spiritual attainment.

---

22. Walton leaves this blank. Hobhouse declares, however, after his analysis of the original autograph of the eighteen rules in the Walton collection in Dr. William's Library, that the words "public houses" (i.e., Coffee Houses) belongs in the blank. See *Selected Mystical Writings*, p. 384.

23. Walton, p. 345-346.

24. Frangois Fenelon, *Christian Perfection* (New York, 1947). Law seldom refers to Fenelon, (1651-1715) but his library at King's Cliffe contained a well-worn copy of the works by that French writer.

Francis de Sales, whom Law also read, wrote *Introduction to the Devout Life* to combat the idea that holiness is possible only for those who live in the seclusion of the cloister.[25] He said, "Wherever we are, we may and ought to aspire to the perfect life."[26] The aim of devotion, he says further, does not consist so much in exterior practice as in the interior dispositions of the heart.[27]

Few writers agree completely on what constitutes Christian perfection, although most admit that it is a limited, or relative perfection—such as may be achieved by man in an imperfect world. Law's early definition, "the right performance of our necessary duties ... in the holy and righteous conduct of ourselves in every state of life," agrees essentially with what Walter Hilton taught about four hundred years earlier. Man ought to strive for the same perfection which Adam knew before the Fall. And to Law, Adamic perfection and angelic perfection were one and the same.

Not every writer on the subject agrees with such a high standard for man. Even John Wesley, who was directly influenced by Law's pronouncements on perfection and who placed perfection principally in man's motives for conduct, does not equate man's perfected state with either Adamic or angelic perfection. Nevertheless, underlying every author's treatment of perfection is a sincere desire to attain, by grace and good works, a flawless state of personal righteousness.

By "right performance of our necessary duties" Law does not refer merely to ritualistic observances or faithful discharge of good works. Neither does he mean withdrawal by man to cloisters or other places of religious retirement to engage in penance and solitary meditation. ". . . the inward piety of the heart and mind, which constitutes the state of Christian perfection, depends upon no outward circumstances.[28] Like Francis de Sales, who aimed to show that true devotion consists principally in the interior disposition of the heart, Law speaks of devotion as "the habit of the mind," the inward state of the heart.[29] Again and again Law emphasizes

---

25. Allan Ross, *Saint Francis de Sales and the Introduction to the Devout Life* (London, 1925), p. 3.
26. Ross, p. 5.
27. Ross, p. 6.
28. *Works*, III, p. 7.
29. Ross, p. 96.

that piety and devotion must involve the totality of one's life before they will be acceptable to God.

In his study of the place of perfection in Christian theology, Flew cites Law as an illustration of those who recalled the Anglican Church to the pursuit of higher objectives than she had sought hitherto.[30] He also tempers his praise for Law with the fear that as guides to devotion, Law's exacting demands on conduct may be depressing to the average worshiper who constantly falls below his ideal, although that ideal is no less attainable than that found in the New Testament.[31]

Those who place Law outside the mainstream of Christian belief because of his "unorthodox views" fail to take into account his clear statements upon key teachings of the Christian church. At no point is he more consonant with the orthodox position than when he depicts scriptural doctrines as the bases for a life of devotion, especially as they apply to the change which must be brought about in man's nature: "All the precepts and doctrines of the gospel are founded on these two great truths: the deplorable corruption of human nature and its new birth in Christ Jesus."[32] As Flew points out, "The kind of perfection which Law expounds is based upon a conversion of man's nature as wrought by God."[33]

Law's devotional predecessors likewise alluded to the Scripture constantly as the basis for transforming their lives: St. Augustine gave himself to diligent study of the Bible as an antidote to heresy and guide to devotion; Jeremy Taylor speaks of the biblical foundation for holy living and holy dying. Even the mystics of the medieval school constantly refer to the scriptural basis for godliness. But Law is more emphatic than most of his predecessors by insisting that the "new birth" is not only a personal religious crisis in which one experiences a momentary "change of heart," but a continuing process of moral renovation as well. He reiterates the necessity of man's participating continuously in this redemptive act which will put him in possession of a new life perfected in God.

---

30. Flew, *The Idea of Perfection in Christian Theology* (London, 1934), p. 293.
31. Flew, p. 301.
32. *Works,* III, p. 13.
33. Flew, *The Idea of Perfection . . .* , p. 294.

When Rufus Jones spoke of Law as "saint" and "prophet" of the soul, he singled out Law from an age of doubt, skepticism and denial.[34] Holding to values far above those of the humanists of his day, Law stood firmly against the anemic pronouncements of the latitudinarians, the profligacy of the libertines, the misuse of reason by the deists, and the denial of miracles by the Socinians.

The reader will find in this book no carefully-plotted allowances for failure in personal devotion. Law's abrupt, probing manner may draw some angry retorts from contemporary readers who contend that their lapses from piety are mere inadvertencies rather than deliberate acts. But Law was not one to make excuses. He penetrated the camouflaged defenses of the apologetic Christian; he believed that bold self-analysis provided the long first step towards spiritual renewal. Truth for this devotionalist *extraordinaire* was not a set of soft-spoken platitudes; happiness for him was to be found only through self-denial, acceptance of divine grace, and emulation of the life of Christ.

* * * * *

The language encountered in this book is Law's own; no attempt is made to tamper with his thought. Words such as "thee", "thou" and "suffer" are modernized, or sections where redundancies occur are deleted. The chapters on "Reading Vain and Impertinent Books" and "The Entertainment of the Stage" are omitted, as they do not seem to be of one piece with the rest of the work.[35] Deleting excessive punctuation and capitalization ought to enhance further this edition of *Christian Perfection*.

---

34. *William Law—Saint of the Eighteenth Century* (New York, 1947), p. 124.
35. The chapter dealing with the stage was first written as a separate pamphlet and not originally prepared as a part of *Christian Perfection.*

I.
The Nature and Necessity
of Christian Perfection

Christian perfection may seem to the average reader to imply some state of life which everyone need not aspire after—that it is made up of such strictness of devotion as is neither necessary nor practicable by Christians generally.

However, I must answer for myself that I know of only one common Christianity which is to be the means of salvation to all men.

If the writers on Christian perfection have fancied to themselves some peculiar degrees of piety or extraordinary devotions which they call by that name, they have not done religion much service by making Christian perfection to consist in anything but the right performance of our necessary duties.

This is the perfection which this treatise endeavors to recommend—a perfection that does not consist in any singular state or condition of life, or in any particular set of duties, but in the holy and religious conduct of ourselves in every state of life. It calls no one to a cloister, but to a full performance of those duties which are necessary for all Christians and common to all states of life.

I call it perfection for two reasons. First, because it represents the height of holiness and purity to which Christianity calls it members. Second, the title may invite the reader to peruse it more diligently, expecting to find not only a discourse upon moral virtues but also a description of those holy dispositions which are the standard of Christian piety.

As this is the highest standard for the Christian to emulate, it is also the lowest degree of holiness which the gospel allows. No order of men can pretend to go higher, yet none can rest in any state of piety that is lower. For if Christian perfection is the right performance of all duties of life in accord with the laws of Christ, what can it be but living in such holy tempers and acting with such dispositions as Christianity requires? If this be perfection, who can exceed it? Yet what state or circumstance of life can allow anyone to fall short of it?

To illustrate this, Christians are to love God with all their heart and all their strength. Can any Christian exceed this? Yet who may be allowed to be defective in it? What is true of the love of God is equally true of all other pious expectations. Consequently all those tempers of the heart which constitute the perfection of Christian piety are equally necessary for all Christians.

As there is but one faith and one baptism, so there is but one piety and one perfection that is common to all Christians.

Some may object that it is as impossible for all people to be equally good as to suppose that all may be equally wise. In a certain sense this is true. For instance, if we define charity as almsgiving or liberal assistance of the poor, then all people may not be equally charitable. But if we understand it to be the habit of mind which stands rightly disposed to all acts of charity, then all people may possess equal charity.

Are not all people to be equally honest, just, true, and faithful? In these virtues all are to be eminent and exact in the same degree. Now as to the external exercise of these duties, there may be a great difference. But as principles of the heart, all may be equally virtuous.

Now this may serve to show us in what respect all people may be equally virtuous, and in what respect they cannot.

A man cannot exercise the spirit of martyrdom until he is brought to the stake. He cannot forgive his enemies until they have done him wrong. He cannot bear poverty and distress until they are brought upon him. Yet he may have a piety and heroic spirit equal to those who have died for the faith. He may have that charity of mind which forgives and prays for its enemies. He may have meekness and resignation to the will of God as disposes people to bear poverty and distress with patience.

It is easy to see, therefore, how persons may differ in instances of goodness and yet be equally good, for the perfection of piety is the perfection of the heart.

Again, people differ in ability. One may possess a more enlightened mind than another, which enables him to see further into his duty and be able to practice it with greater exactness. Yet if another is as true and faithful to that measure of light and knowledge which God has given him, he is as good a man as he who is true and faithful to a greater light.

We can hardly reconcile it with divine goodness to give one man two talents and another five unless we suppose he is as high in his master's pleasure who makes right use of two as he who makes right use of five talents.

It is the perfection of the heart that makes the perfection of every state of life.

Again, some may object that the different degrees of glory in another life supposes that good men differ in their degrees of goodness in this life. But this is no proof that all men are not called to the same goodness and perfection. The best of men do not always perform their duties as well as they might have any more than they do the less good. Differences in their failings may make them objects of God's different rewards, though the rule from which they failed was common to them all.

Some may also say that if there are different degrees of glory, this shows that men may be saved and happy without aspiring after the perfection to which they are called. While some may be admitted to happiness though they have not attained to all the perfection to which they were called, yet it does not follow that any people will be saved who did not strive after that perfection. It is a very different case to fall short of our perfection after our best endeavors and to stop short of it by not attempting to arrive at it. The one practice may carry men to a high reward in heaven and the other cast them with the unprofitable servant into outer darkness.

Though God gives different rewards, it is not in man's power to take them of himself. It is not for anyone to say, "I will practice so much goodness and take such a reward." God sees different abilities and frailties in men. Because of His mercy He may accept a lower state of piety on the part of some than others. Though such a state of piety *may* be accepted, yet it ceases to be that state as soon as one has chosen it. All Christians are called to one and the same perfection and are equally obliged to labor after it.

II.
Man's Loss of Paradise

The wisdom of mankind has for ages been inquiring into the nature of man and of the world in which he is placed. The wants and miseries of human nature and the vanity of worldly enjoyments have made it difficult for the wisest man to tell what human happiness was or wherein it consisted. It has pleased the infinite goodness of God to satisfy all our wants and inquiries by a revelation made to the world by His Son, Jesus Christ.

This revelation has laid open the great secrets of Providence, explained the present state of things, and given man all the information that is necessary to quiet his anxieties, content him with his condition, and lead him safely to everlasting rest and happiness.

It is now only necessary that the poor wisdom of man does not exalt itself against God, that we allow our eyes to be opened to Him who made them, and that our lives be conducted by Him in whom "we live, and move, and have our being."[1]

Light is now come into the world, but men must be willing to come out of darkness. As happiness is the sole end of our labors, so this divine revelation aims at nothing else. It shows us the true state of our condition, both our vanity and excellence, our greatness and manners, our felicity and misery.

Before this, man was a mere riddle to himself and his condition full of darkness and perplexity. But this light has dispersed all of his anxiety. It has acquainted him with God by adding heaven to earth,

---

1. Acts 17:28

and eternity to time and has opened such a glorious view of things as makes man, even in his present condition, full of a peace of God which passes all understanding.

This revelation teaches us that we have a spirit within us that was created after the divine image, that this spirit is now in a fallen, corrupt condition, that the body in which it is placed is its grave where it is enslaved to fleshly thoughts, blinded with false notions of good and evil, and dead to all relish of its true happiness.

It teaches us that the world in which we live is also in a disordered state and cursed for the sake of man—it is no longer the paradise that God made it, but the remains of a drowned world full of marks of God's displeasure and the sin of its inhabitants.

The excellency, therefore, of the Christian religion appears in this: it puts an end to this state of things, blots out all ideas of worldly wisdom, and creates all anew. It calls man from an earthly life and earthly conversation to be born again of the Holy Spirit and to be made a member of the kingdom of God.

It crushes into nothing the concerns of this life, condemns it as a state of vanity and darkness, and leads man to a happiness with God in the regions of light.

It proposes the purification of our souls, the enlivening us with the Divine Spirit. It sets before us new goods and evils and forms us to a glorious participation of the divine nature.

This is the sole end of Christianity: to lead us from all thoughts of rest and repose here, to separate us from worldly tempers, to deliver us from the folly of our passions, and to unite us to God, the true fountain of all good. The mighty change which Christianity aims at, then, is to put us into a new state, reform our whole natures, purify our souls and make them the inhabitants of heavenly and immortal bodies.

III.
Man Made for Two Worlds

The manner by which the whole state of things is changed and we are raised to a union with God is equally great and wonderful. "I am the way, the truth, and the life," said our Lord, "no man cometh unto the Father but by me."[1] As all things were at first created by the Son of God, so are all things restored and redeemed by the same divine person.

The price and dignity of this redemption at once confounds the pride and relieves the misery of man. How fallen must he be from God, how disordered and odious his nature that he should need so great a mediator to recommend his repentance. And on the other hand, how comforting that so high a method, so stupendous a means, should be taken to restore him to a state of peace and favor with God.

This is the point of view in which every Christian is to behold himself. He is to overlook the poor projects of human life and consider himself as a creature through his natural corruption falling into a state of endless misery, but by the mercy of God redeemed to a state of everlasting felicity.

All the precepts and doctrines of the gospel are founded on these two great truths: the deplorable corruption of human nature and its new birth in Christ Jesus. One includes all the misery, and the other all the happiness of man.

The corruption of our nature makes mortification, self-denial, and the death of our bodies necessary. Human nature must be altered; flesh and blood must be changed before it can enter the Kingdom of Heaven. Our new birth makes the reception of God's

---

1. John 14:6

Spirit necessary to form us to that life to which the resurrection of Jesus Christ has entitled us.

If we would think and live like Christians, we must act suitably to these terms of our condition—fearing and avoiding all the motions of our corrupted nature, cherishing the secret inspiration of the Holy Spirit, opening our minds for the reception of the Divine Light, and pressing after all the graces and perfections of our new birth.

We must conform to this double capacity: to fear and watch and pray like men who are always in danger of eternal death and to believe, hope, labor, and aspire like Christians who are called to "fight the good fight of faith" and "lay hold on eternal life."[2] This knowledge of ourselves makes human life a state of infinite importance, placed upon a dreadful point between two eternities.

Had we been made only for this world, worldly wisdom had been our highest wisdom; but as Chritianity has redeemed us to a contrary state, worldly wisdom is now our greatest foolishness. It is now our only wisdom to understand our new state aright and to conduct ourselves by the principles of our redemption.

IV.
The Glory of Man's New Estate

The Christian state is an invisible life in the Spirit of God, supported not by sensible goods, but by the spiritual graces of faith and hope. The natural man, especially while busied in earthly cares and enjoyments, easily forgets the great and heavenly condition in which religion places him.

In God "we live, and move, and have our being."[1] He is the "Lamb slain from the foundation of the world,"[2] the true light that

---

2. I Timothy 6:12   1. Acts 17:28   2. Revelation 13:8

"lighteth every man that cometh into the world."[3] He is the *alpha* and *omega,* the beginning and end of all things. The whole creation subsists in Him and by Him. But how faintly do we sense these great truths!

The Apostle tells us that we Christians are "come unto Mount Zion, and unto the city of the living God, to the heavenly Jerusalem, and to an innumerable company of angels and to the general assembly of the first-born, which are written in heaven and to God the Judge of all, and to the spirits of just men made perfect, and to Jesus the mediator of a new covenant . . . ."[4] But our senses see or feel nothing of this state of glory; they only show us a society among vain and worldly men, laboring and contending for the poor enjoyments of a vain world.

We are the temples of the Holy Spirit, members of Christ's mystical body, of His flesh and of His bones, receiving life, spirit, and motion from Him, our Head. But our senses, the maxims of this life, and the spirit of the world teach quite another turn of mind: to enjoy the good things of life, to seek after riches and honors, and to dread nothing so much as poverty, disgrace, and persecution. Well may this life be deemed a state of darkness since it obscures all the true appearance of things and keeps our minds insensible to matters of infinite moment.

Our Savior prayed for all His followers, "that they all may be one, as Thou, Father, art in me, and I in Thee; that they also may be one in us . . . And the glory which Thou gavest me I have given them, that they may be one, even as we are one. I in them and thou in me, that they may be made perfect in one."[5] Happy is he who has ears to hear and a heart to feel the majesty and glory of this description of our new life in Christ!

Surely if we understood what our Lord conceived when He sent up this prayer to God, our hearts would be always praying and our souls ever aspiring after this state of perfection, this union with Christ in God.

The Apostle tells us that "we have borne the image of the earthly, we shall also bear the image of the heavenly."[6] And that when Christ,

---

3. John 1:9   4. Hebrews 12:22   5. John 17:21   6. I Corinthians 15:49

"who is our life, shall appear, then shall ye also appear with Him in glory.[7]

St. John said, "Beloved, now are we the sons of God, and it does not yet appear what we shall be; but we know that when he shall appear, we shall be like him, for we shall see him as he is."[8] The apostle's conclusion is "and every man that hath this hope in him purifieth himself even as he is pure."[9] This lesson teaches us that no man can be said to have this hope in him unless he shows it by such a purification of himself as may resemble the purity of Christ.

If we would conceive our true state, our real good and evil, we must with the eyes of faith penetrate into the invisible world, the world of spirits, and consider our order and condition among them—a world, as St. John says, "that has no need of the sun, neither of the moon to shine upon it, for the glory of God doth lighten it . . . ."[10] It is there that we must take an eternal fellowship or fall into a kingdom of darkness and everlasting misery.

Christianity is so divine in nature, so noble in its ends, so extensive in its views, that it has no lesser subjects than these to entertain our thoughts. It buries our bodies, burns the present world, triumphs over death by a general resurrection, and opens all into an eternal state.

It never considers us in any other respect than as fallen spirits. It disregards the distinctions of human society, and proposes nothing to our fears but eternal misery and nothing to our hopes but an endless enjoyment of the divine nature.

Take upon you. therefore, a spirit suitable to this exalted state. Remember that you are an eternal spirit, that you are for a few months and years in a state of flesh and blood only to test whether you will be forever happy with God or fall into everlasting misery with the devil.

---

7. Colossians 3:4   8. I John 3:2   9. I John 3:3   10. Revelation 21:23

V.
The Vanity of Worldly Enjoyments

You will often hear of other concerns and other greatness in this world. You will see every order of men pursuing some fancied happiness of their own. But when you see this state of human life, fancy that you see all the world asleep—the prince no longer a prince, the beggar no longer begging, but every man sleeping out of his proper state, some happy, others tormented—and all changing their condition as fast as one dream can succeed another. When you have seen this, you have seen all that the world awake can do for you. If you will, you may go to sleep for awhile and dream. For when you are as happy as the world can make you, all is but sleeping and dreaming, and what is still worse, it is like sleeping in a ship when one ought to be redeeming himself from slavery.

This is no inordinate excess of melancholy, but a sober reflection justly suited to the vanity of worldly enjoyments. For if the doctrines of Christianity are true, if you are that fallen spirit, that immortal nature which religion teaches us, if you are to meet death, resurrection, and judgment as the forerunners of an eternal state, what are all the little flashes of pleasure, the changing appearance of worldly felicities but so many sorts of dreams?

Is the beggar asleep when he imagines he is building himself fine houses, or the prisoner in a dream when he fancies himself free in open fields and fine groves? And can you think that your immortal spirit is awake when it is delighting itself in the shadows and trifles of worldly happiness?

If it be true that man is upon his trial, if the trial is for eternity, if life is but a vapor, what is there that deserves serious thought but how to get out of the world and make a right passage to our eternal state?

Indeed the littleness and insignificance of the boasted honors of human life appear sufficiently from the things themselves without comparing them to the subjects of religion.

Ahasuerus, the great prince of the eastern world, put a question to Haman, his chief minister of state: "What shall be done unto the man whom the king delighteth to honor?"[1]

Haman, imagining that he was the person whom the king had in his thoughts, answered:

> Let the royal apparel be brought which the king useth to wear and the horse that the king rideth upon and the crown royal which is set upon his head; and let this apparel and horse be delivered to the hand of one of the king's most noble princes, that they may array the man withal, whom the king delighteth to honor, and bring him on horseback through the street of the city, and proclaim before him, thus shall it be done to the man whom the king delighteth to honor.[2]

Here you see the sum total of worldly honors. An ambitious Haman cannot think of anything greater to ask; Ahasuerus, the greatest monarch in the world, has nothing greater to give to his greatest favorite. Powerful as he is, he can only give such honors as these. Yet these are the mighty things for which men forget God, forget their immortality, forget the difference between an eternity in heaven and an eternity in hell. There needs no great understanding, no mighty depth of thought to see through the vanity of all such worldly enjoyments.

It is the manner of some countries, in the burial of their dead, to put a staff and shoes and money in the grave along with the corpse. We justly censure the folly and ignorance of such a practice to assist the dead; but if we did but as truly understand what life is, we should see as much to ridicule in the poor contrivances to assist the living.

How many things in life do people labor after which, when gotten, are as much real use to them as a staff and shoes to a corpse underground?

This is not carrying matters too far, for the value of worldly riches and honors can no more be too much bemeaned than the riches and

---

1. Esther 6:6   2. Esther 6:8,9

greatness of the other life can be too much exalted. We don't cheat ourselves out of any real happiness by looking upon all worldly honors as transitory any more than we cheat ourselves by securing honors that are solid and eternal. There is no happiness lost by not being great and rich.

He who condemns *all* the external show and state of life as equally vain is no more deceived or carried to too great a contempt for the things of this life than he who only condemns the vainest things. If we remember that the whole race of mankind is a race of fallen spirits that pass through the world as an arrow passes through the air, we will soon perceive that all things here are equally great and small.

If we but see ourselves in the light which Christ has brought into the world, we will see that nothing concerns us but what concerns an everlasting spirit that is going to God, that there are no enjoyments here that are worth a thought but those that make us more perfect in those holy tempers which will carry us to heaven.

VI.
A New Nature Required

Christianity is not a school for teaching moral virtue, or polishing our manners, or forming us to live in the world with decency and gentility. It is deeper in its designs and much nobler in its ends. It implies an entire change of life, a dedication of our souls and bodies unto God in the strictest and highest sense of the words.

Our Savior came into the world not to divide things between heaven and earth, but to make war with every state of life, to put an end to the designs of flesh and blood, and to show us that we must either leave this world to become sons of God, or by enjoying it to take our portion among devils and damned spirits.

Death is not more certainly a separation of our souls from our bodies than the Christian life is a separation of our souls from worldly dispositions, vain indulgences, and unnecessary cares.

No sooner are we converted to Christ but we are to consider ourselves as new and holy persons who are entered upon a new state of things, and who have renounced all to be fellow-heirs with Christ and members of His kingdom.

There is no alteration of life, no change of condition that implies half so much as the alteration which Christianity introduces. It is a kingdom of heaven begun upon earth, and by being made members of it, we are entered into a new state of goods and evils.

Eternity alters the face and nature of everything in this world. Life is only a trial. Prosperity becomes adversity, pleasure a mischief and nothing a good but as it increases our hope, purifies our natures, and prepares us to receive higher degrees of happiness.

Let us now see what it is to enter into this state of redemption.

Our own church, in conformity with Scripture and the practice of tradition, makes it necessary for us to renounce pomps and vanities of the world before we can be received as members of Christian communion.[1] Whenever we yield ourselves to the pleasures, profits, and honors of this life, we turn apostates, break our covenant with God, and go back from the express conditions on which we were admitted into the communion of Christ's Church.

If we consult either the life or doctrines of our Lord, we shall find that Christianity is a covenant that contains only the terms of changing and resigning this world for another that is to come. It is a state of things that wholly regards eternity and knows of no other goods and evils but such as relate to another life.

It is a kingdom of heaven that has no other interests in this world than as it takes its members out of it, and when the number of the elect is complete, this world will be consumed with fire as having no other reason for existence than furnishing members for that blessed society which is to last forever.

I cannot here omit observing the folly and vanity of human wisdom which pleases itself with its mighty prosperities and lasting es-

---

1. Law refers here to the Anglican Church, of which he was a member.

tablishments in a world doomed to destruction, and which is to last no longer than the time when a sufficient number are redeemed out of it.

Christianity is, therefore, a course of holy discipline solely fitted to the cure and recovery of fallen spirits and intends such a change in our nature as may raise us to a nearer union with God and qualify us for such higher degrees of happiness.

That Christianity requires a change of nature, a new life perfectly devoted to God, is plain from the spirit and tenor of the gospel. Our Lord said, "Except a man be born again of water and of the spirit, he cannot enter into the kingdom of God."[2] We are told that "to as many as received Him, to them He gave power to become the sons of God . . . which were born not of blood nor of the will of the flesh nor of the will of man, but of God."[3]

These words plainly teach us that Christianity implies some great changes of nature—that as our birth was to us the beginning of a new life and brought us into a society of earthly enjoyments, so Christianity is another birth that brings us into a condition altogether as new as when we first saw the light. We enter upon fresh terms of life, have new relations, new hopes and fears, and an entire change of everything that can be called good or evil.

This principle of a new life is the very essence and soul of Christianity; it is the seal of the promises, the mark of our sonship, the earnest of our inheritance, the security of our hope, and the foundation of all our acceptance with God. "He that is in Christ," said the Apostle, "is a new creature . . . ."[4]

No number of moral virtues, no partial obedience, no modes of worship, no external acts of adoration, no articles of faith make us true Christians. There must be a new principle of life. "If the Spirit of Him that raised up Jesus from the dead dwell in you, He that raised up Christ from the dead shall also quicken your mortal bodies by His spirit that dwelleth in you."[5] "For as many as are led by the Spirit of God, they are the sons of God."[6]

Since the Scriptures require a life suitable to the spirit and manner of Jesus Christ, since they do not permit us to be sons of God

---

2. John 3:5   3. John 1:12,13   4. II Corinthians 5:17   5. Romans 8:11   6. Romans 8:14

unless we live and act according to the spirit of God, it is past doubt that Christianity requires an entire change of nature and a life perfectly devoted to God. For what can imply a greater change than from a carnal to a spiritual mind? What can be more contrary to the works of the Spirit than the works of the flesh? It is the difference of heaven and hell.

Light and darkness are but faint resemblances of that great contrariety that is between the spirit of God and the spirit of the world. Its wisdom is foolishness, its friendship is enmity with God.

"All that is in the world, the lust of the flesh, the lust of the eyes, and the pride of life, is not of the Father . . . ."[7] Worldly opinions, proud reasonings, fleshly cares, and earthly concerns are all so many false judgments—mere lies, and we know who is the father of lies.

For this reason the Scripture makes the devil the god and prince of this world because the spirit which reigns there is entirely from him, and so far as we are governed by the wisdom and spirit of the world, so far are we governed by that evil power of darkness.

If we would see more of this contrariety and the change our new life in Christ implies, let us consider further what it means to be born of God.

St. John tells us one sure mark of our new birth when he says, "whatsoever is born of God overcometh the world."[8] The new birth, or the Christian life, is considered as opposition to the world and all that is in it—its vain cares, its false glories, its proud designs, its sensual pleasures. If we have overcome these so as to be governed by other cares, other glories, other designs, and other pleasures, then we are born of God. Then is the wisdom of this world and the friendship of this world turned into the wisdom and friendship of God, which will forever keep us "heirs of God and joint-heirs with Christ."[9]

---

7. I John 2:16   8. I John 5:4   9. Romans 8:17

VII.
Without Sinful Intention

The same apostle helps us to another sign of our new life in God: "Whosoever is born of God doth not commit sin, for his seed remaineth in him and he cannot sin because he is born of God."[1]

This is not to be understood as if he who was born of God was in an absolute state of perfection and incapable afterwards of falling into anything that was sinful. It only means that he who is born of God is possessed of a principle and spirit that makes him utterly hate and avoid all sin. He is said not to commit sin in the sense that a man may be said not to do that which is his constant care to prevent. He cannot sin as it may be said of a man who has no principle but covetousness cannot do things that are expensive, because it is his constant care to be sparing, and if he incur expense, it is contrary to his intention, and he returns to saving with double diligence.

Such is he who is born of God. Purity and holiness is his only aim, and he is more incapable of having any sinful intentions than the miser is of generous expense, and if he finds himself in any sin, it is his greatest pain and trouble, and he strives after holiness with a double zeal.

To be born of God is to have a mind so entirely devoted to purity and holiness that it may be said of us in a just sense that we cannot commit sin. When holiness is such a habit of our minds as to govern all our ambitions and actions without the intrusion of any other principle, then we are alive in God and living members of the mystical body of His Son, Jesus Christ.

This is the true standard by which we are to judge ourselves. We

---

1. I John 3:9

are not true Christians unless we are born of God, and we are not born of God unless it can be said of us in this sense that we cannot commit sin. When by an inward principle of holiness we stand so disposed to all degrees of virtue as the ambitious man stands disposed to all steps of greatness, when we hate and avoid all kinds of sins and the covetous man hates and avoids all sorts of loss and expense, then we are such sons of God as cannot commit sin.

We must, therefore, examine the state and temper of our minds to see whether we are thus changed in our natures, whether we be so spiritual as to have overcome the world, so holy that we cannot commit sin. Since this is the undeniable doctrine of Scripture, we ought to consider it as necessary to salvation as initially believing in Jesus Christ.

To be eminent for any particular virtue or to detest and avoid several kinds of sins is nothing at all. But when the temper of our soul is entirely changed, when we are renewed in the spirit of our minds and are full of relish and desire of all goodness, of fear and abhorrence of all evil, then, as St. John speaks, "we may know that we are of the truth and shall assure our hearts before Him . . . then shall we know that He abideth in us by the Spirit which He hath given us.'[2]

Two marks, therefore, of those who are born of God are: they have overcome the world, and they do not commit sin.

To these I shall add only a third, which is given to us by Christ Himself, "I say unto you, love your enemies, bless them that curse you, do good to them that hate you, and pray for them which despitefully use you and persecute you, that you may be the children of your Father which is in heaven."[3]

It is not enough, therefore, that we love our friends and benefactors, but we must love like God if we will show that we are born of Him. We must, like Him, have a universal love and tenderness for all mankind, imitating that love which would that all men should be saved.

God is love, and this we are to observe as the true standard for ourselves, that "he who dwelleth in God dwelleth in love."[4] Consequently, he who dwells not in love dwells not in God. It is impossible,

---

therefore, to be a true Christian and an enemy at the same time.

Mankind has no enemy but the devil, and those who partake of his malicious spirit.

There is perhaps no duty of religion that is so contrary to flesh and blood as this, but as difficult as it may seem to a worldly mind, it is still necessary and will easily be performed by those who are in Christ.

Let us contemplate the height and depth of Christian holiness and that godlike spirit which our religion requires. The duty of universal love and benevolence, even to our bitterest enemies, may serve to convince us that to be Christians we must be born again, change our very nature, and have no governing desire of our souls but that of being made like God.

We cannot exercise or delight in this duty until we delight only in increasing our likeness to God. Be assured, Christianity does not consist in any partial amendment of our lives, but in an entire change of our natural selves and a life wholly devoted to God.

This same doctrine is again taught by our Lord when speaking of little children, He said, "Suffer [them] to come unto me, for of such is the kingdom of God." and again, "Whosoever shall not receive the kingdom of God as a little child shall in no wise enter therein."[5]

One characteristic of infants is that they have everything to learn. They are to be taught by others what they are to hope for and fear and wherein their proper happiness consists. It is in this sense that we are chiefly to become as infants, to be as though we had everything to learn and to allow ourselves to be taught what we are to choose and what to avoid, to pretend to no wisdom of our own, but to be ready to pursue that happiness which God in Christ proposes to us, and to accept it with childlike simplicity without opposition.

The wisdom of this world, the intrigues of life, the designs of greatness and ambition lead to another kingdom, and he who would follow Christ must empty himself of this vanity and put on the meek ornaments of infant and undesigning simplicity.

"Where is the wise? Where is the scribe? Where is the disputer of

---

5. Luke 18:16,17

this world?" says the Apostle. "Hath not God made foolish the wisdom of this world?"[6]

If, therefore, we will partake of the wisdom of God, we must think and judge of this world and its most boasted gifts as the wisdom of God judges them. We must deem them foolishness and with undivided hearts labor after one wisdom, one perfection, one happiness in being entirely devoted to God.

VIII.
Baptism into His Death

The Holy Spirit convinces us of the same truth by speaking of it as a state of death. Thus says the apostle, "Ye are dead, and your life is hid with Christ in God."[1] That is, we Christians are dead to this world, and the life we now live is not to be reckoned by any visible or worldly goods, but is hid in Christ; it is a spiritual enjoyment, a life of faith and not of sight. We are members of that mystical body of which Christ is the head. We are entered into a kingdom that is not of this world. And in this state of death are we as Christians to continue until Christ comes.

To show us that this death begins with our Christian state, we are said to be "buried with him in baptism." As the Apostle says, "Know ye not that so many of us as were baptized into Jesus Christ were baptized into his death? Therefore, we are buried with him by baptism into death."[2]

Christians may be said to be baptized into the death of Christ if their baptism puts them into a state like that of our Savior at His death. Christian baptism is not only an external rite by which we enter into the external society of Christ's Church, but it is a solemn

---

6. I Corinthians 1:20   1. Colossians 3:3   2. Romans 6:3,4

consecration which presents us as an offering to God, as Christ was offered at His death.

We are, therefore, no longer alive to the enjoyments of this world, but as Christ was then nailed to the cross and given over entirely to God that He might be made "perfect through suffering"[3] and ascend to the right hand of God, so is our old man to be crucified and we consecrated to God by a conformity to the death of Christ. As Christ was raised from the dead, even so we should also walk in newness of life, and being risen with Christ, should seek those things which are above.

This is the true state of Christianity. Baptism does not make us effectual Christians unless it brings us into a state of death, consecrates us to God, and begins a life suitable to that state of things to which our Savior is risen from the dead. Only this is the holiness of the Christian life which implies such a resignation of mind, such a dedication of ourselves as may resemble the death of Christ, and on the other hand such a newness of life, such an ascension of the soul, such a holy and heavenly behavior as may show that we are risen with Christ and belong to that glorious state where He now sits at the right hand of God.

It is in this sense that Jesus says of His disciples, "they are not of this world, even as I am not of this world."[4] Not being left to live the life of the world, but chosen out of it for the purposes of His kingdom, they were to copy after His death and oblation of Himself to God.

This is the condition of all Christians until the consummation of all things. They are to carry on the same designs and by the same means raise out of this corrupted state a number of fellow-heirs with Christ in everlasting glory. The Savior of the world has purchased mankind with His blood, not to live in ease and pleasurable enjoyments, not to spend time in softness and luxury or in the gratification of pride, idleness and vanity, but to drink of His cup, to be baptized with the baptism that He was baptized with, to make war with their corrupt natures, to humble themselves and, like Him, be made perfect through sufferings.

St. Paul speaks of the benefits of Christ's resurrection when he

---

3. Hebrews 2:10   4. John 17:16

says, "That I may know him and the power of his resurrection, and the fellowship of his sufferings, being made conformable to his death."[5] It is being made conformable to His death on which he founds his hopes of sharing in the resurrection of Christ. If Christians think that salvation is now to be had on softer terms and that a life of indulgence and sensual gratifications is consistent with the terms of the gospel, they are miserably blind and as much mistake their Savior as the Jews who expected a temporal messiah to deliver them.

Our redemption is a redemption by sacrifice, and none are redeemed but they who conform to it. "If we suffer [with Him], we shall also reign with Him."[6]

We must, then, if we would be wise unto salvation, die and rise again like Christ and make all the actions of our lives holy by offering them to God. Whether we eat or drink or whatever we do, we must do all to the glory of God.

If this is Christian piety, it may serve to instruct at least two sorts of people. First, those who are content with an outward decency and regularity of life—those who are content with an outward form of behavior without that newness of heart and spirit which the gospel requires.

Charity, chastity, sobriety, and justice may be practiced without Christian piety. A heathen may be charitable and temperate, but to make these virtues become parts of Christian piety, they must proceed from a heart truly turned unto God. Temperance and justice without this turn of heart are not Christian until they proceed from a true Christian spirit.

A Christian must be sober, charitable and just upon the same principles and with the same spirit that he receives the Holy Sacrament. As the eating of bread and drinking of wine are of no use to us without those religious dispositions which constitute the true frame of a pious mind, so is it the same in all other duties. They are mere outward ceremonies and useless actions unless they are performed in the spirit of religion.

This doctrine may also instruct a second group: those who are

---

5. Philippians 3:10   6. II Timothy 2:12

complete strangers to what they must do to become true Christians. Some who are ashamed of the folly of their lives and who begin to look towards religion think they have done enough when they alter the outward course of their lives, abate some of their extravagances, or become careful of some particular virtue.

Thus, a man whose life has been a course of folly thinks he has made a sufficient change by becoming temperate. Another imagines he has sufficiently reformed by not neglecting the public worship as he used to. But such people should consider that religion does not consist in the fewness of our vices or in any particular amendment of our lives, but in such a thorough change of heart as makes piety and holiness the measure and rule of all our lives.

Let them remember that they who measure themselves by themselves are not wise. Let them remember that they are not disciples of Christ until they have, like Him, offered their whole body and soul.

Nothing less than this great change of heart and mind can give anyone any assurance that he is truly turned to God. There is this one term of salvation, "He that is in Christ is a new creature."[7] How insignificant all other attainments are is shown in the following words: "Many will say to me in that day, Lord, Lord, have we not prophesied in thy name? And in thy name cast out devils? And in thy name have done many wonderful works? And then will I profess unto them, I never knew you. Depart from me, ye that work iniquity."[8]

Let us, therefore, look carefully to ourselves and consider what manner of spirit we are. Let us not think our condition safe because we are of this or that church or because we are strict observers of the external practices of religion, for these are marks that belong outside the Christian standard. All are not Christ's who prophesy or even work miracles in His name.

If religion has raised us into a new world, if it has filled us with new ends of life, if it has taken possession of our hearts and altered the whole turn of our minds and taught us to live by the realities of an invisible world, then may we humbly hope that we are true followers of

---

7. II Corinthians 5:17　　　　　8. Matthew 7:22,23

the holy Jesus, and as such may rejoice in the day of Christ "that [we] have neither run in vain, nor labored in vain."[9]

IX.
Renunciation of the World

The Christian religion which aims to raise a new, spiritual, and as yet invisible world, and to place man in a certain order among thrones, prinicpalities, and spiritual beings, is at entire enmity with this present, corrupt state of flesh and blood. It ranks the present world along with the flesh and the devil as an equal enemy to those glorious ends and that perfection of human nature which our redemption proposes.

The gospel lays its first foundation in the renunciation of the world as a state of false goods and enjoyments which feed the vanity and corruption of our nature, fill our hearts with foolish and wicked passions, and keep us separate from God, the only source of happiness.

"My kingdom," says our Lord, "is not of this world."[1] A further representation of the distinction that exists between this kingdom and the concerns of the world follows:

A certain man made a great supper and bade many and sent his servant at supper time to say to them that were bidden: come, for all things are now ready; and they all with one consent began to make excuse. The first said, I have bought a piece of ground and I must needs go and see it. Another said, I have bought five yoke of oxen, and I go to prove them; I pray thee have me excused. Another said, I have married a wife, and therefore I cannot come.[2]

---

9 Philippians 2:16   1. John 18:36   2. Luke 14:16-20

We find that the master of the house was angry and said, "None of those men which were bidden shall taste of my supper."[3] Our Savior a little afterwards applies it all in this manner, "Whosoever he be of you that forsaketh not all that he hath, he cannot be my disciple."[4]

It is no more pardonable to be less affected by the things of religion for the sake of any worldly business than for the indulgence of our pride or any other passion. Christianity is a calling that puts an end to all other callings. We are no longer to consider it as our proper state or employment to take care of oxen, look after an estate, or attend to the most plausible affairs of life, but to reckon every condition as equally trifling and fit to be neglected for the sake of the one thing needful.

Men of serious business and management generally censure those who trifle away their time in idle and impertinent pleasures. But they don't consider that attention to business in which they are skilled may get hold of the heart and render man as vain and odious in the sight of God as any other gratification. Though they may call it an honest care, a creditable industry, or any other plausible name, yet it is their particular gratification and a wisdom that can no more recommend itself to the eyes of God than the wisdom of an epicure.

The wisdom of this world gives an importance and air of greatness to several ways of life and ridicules others as vain and contemptible, but the wisdom from above condemns all labor as equally fruitless except that which labors after everlasting life.

Though we distinguish between cares and pleasures, yet if we would speak exactly, it is pleasure alone that governs and moves us in every state of life. And the man who in the business of the world would be thought to pursue it because of its use and importance is as much governed by his taste for pleasures as he who studies the gratification of his sensual desires. For there is no wisdom or reason in anything but religion, nor is any way of life less vain than another but as it is made serviceable to piety and conspires with the designs of our faith to raise mankind to a participation and enjoyment of the divine nature.

---

3. Luke 14:24   4. Luke 14:33

Therefore our Savior calls men equally from the cares of employments as from the pleasures of their senses, because they are equally wrong if misused. They equally nourish the corruption of our nature and are equally nothing when compared to that high state of glory which by His sufferings and death He has merited for us.

Let the ambitious man but show the folly and irregularity of covetousness, and the same reasons will show the folly and irregularity of ambition.

Let the man who is deep in worldly business but show the vanity and shame of a life that is devoted to pleasures and the same reasons will as fully set forth the vanity of worldly cares, so that whoever can condemn sensuality, ambition, or any way of life upon the principles of reason and religion carries his own condemnation within his own breast. Worldly cares are no more holy and virtuous than worldly pleasures. They are as great a mistake in life, and when they divide or possess the heart, they are equally vain and shameful as any sensual gratification.

It is granted that some cares are made necessary by the necessities of nature; the same may also be observed of some pleasures. The pleasures of eating, drinking, and rest are equally necessary. But if religion and reason do not limit these pleasures, we fall from rational creatures into gluttons and epicures. In like manner, our care after some worldly things is necessary, but if this care is not bounded by the just wants of nature, if it fills the mind with false desires and cravings, it is vain and irregular.

For this reason our Lord points His doctrines at the most common employments to teach us that they may occupy our minds inordinately and distract us far from our true good. He calls us from such cares to convince us that even the necessities of life must be sought with a kind of indifference. How much do Christians generally vary from this ideal!

Christianity commands us "to take no thought, saying, What shall we eat? or, What shall we drink?"[5] Yet Christians are restless till they can eat sumptuously. They are to be indifferent about rainment, but they are full of concern about fine array. They are to

---

5. Matthew 6:31

take no thought for the morrow, yet many of them think they have lived in vain if they are not able to leave large estates when they die.

It must not be said that there is some defect in these doctrines, or that they are not plainly enough taught in the Scriptures because the lives and behavior of Christians are so contrary to them.

X.
The Unchanging Quality of Holiness

I know it is pretended by some that these doctrines of our Savior concerning "forsaking all" related only to His first followers, that the first Christians differed from us in certain respects. They were personally called to follow Christ; they received particular commissions from Him; they were empowered to work miracles and called to a certain expectation of suffering in the world.

But it is to be observed that this difference in the state of the Church is a difference in the external state and not in the inward state of Christians; it is a difference that relates to the affairs and conditions of the world and not to personal holiness.

The world may sometimes favor Christianity; at other times it may oppose it with persecution. This change of the world makes two different states of the Church without making any difference in the inward personal holiness of Christians, which is to be always the same whether the world smiles or frowns upon it.

Humility, meekness, heavenly affection, devotion, charity and a contempt for the world are all internal qualities of personal holiness. They constitute the spirit of religion which is required for its own excellence and is, therefore, of constant and eternal obligation. There is always the same fitness and reasonableness in them, the same perfection in the practicing of them, and the same rewards always due to them.

We must, therefore, look carefully into the nature of things which we find were required of the first Christians. We find that they were called to sufferings at the hands of other people, which may not be our case. But if we see they are called to sufferings by their own choice, to voluntary self-denials and renunciation of their own rights, we may judge amiss if we think this was their particular duty as the first disciples of Christ. These sufferings are as truly parts of personal holiness and devotion as any instances of charity, humility, and love of God that can possibly be supposed.

And it will be difficult to show why all Christians are now obliged to imitate Christ in meekness and lowliness of heart if they, like the first Christians, are not obliged to follow Him in the instances of self-denial.

Let us not deceive ourselves. The gospel preaches the same doctrine to us that our Savior taught His first disciples, and though it may not call us to the same external state of the Church, yet it infallibly calls us to the same inward holiness and newness of life. It is out of all question that this renunciation of the world was then required because of its suitableness to the spirit of Christianity if we are not obliged to be equally holy, to act upon the same high principles of devotion, and to disregard earthly goods.

Our Lord's Sermon on the Mount may as well be confined to His first disciples when He said, "Ye cannot serve God and mammon"[1] as when He said, "Whosoever . . . forsaketh not all that he hath, cannot be my disciple."[2] Let anyone think he can find the least shadow of a reason why Christians should at first be called to a higher degree of heavenly affection, devotion to God, and disregard of the world than they are now, and it will be easy to show that they were obliged to a stronger faith, a livelier hope than they are now.

However, if faith and hope are graces of too excellent a nature and too essential to the life and spirit of a Christian to admit of any abatements in any age of the Church, I should think that heavenly affection, devotion to God, and dying to the world are characteristics equally essential to the spirit of religion and too necessary to the perfection of the soul to be less required in one age than in another.

---

1. Matthew 6:24   2. Luke 14:33

All men will readily grant that it would be very absurd to suppose that more articles of faith should have been necessary to be believed by our Savior's first followers than by Christians of after ages. Is it not absurd to suppose that these articles of faith should not have always the same relation to salvation? Is it not equally absurd to suppose the same of any graces or virtues of the soul?

I believe everyone will readily grant that whenever the Church falls into persecution as was in the beginning, we are then to suffer as the first Christians did. The reasons are: what they did was right; their example was agreeable to the doctrine of Christ; our lives are no more valuable then theirs; suffering for the faith is always entitled to the same reward.

If it can be shown that the world is changed, that its enjoyments have not that contrariety to the spirit of Christianity that they had in the apostles' days, there may be some grounds for Christians today to take some other methods than they did. But if the world is the same enemy it was at first, if its wisdom is still foolishness, its friendship still enmity with God, we are as much obliged to treat this enemy as the first disciples of Christ did.

XI.
Perfection Minus One

Our Lord gave as a general term of Christianity, "Whosoever he be of you that forsaketh not all that he hath, he cannot be my disciple."[1] St. Mark tells us:

There came one running and kneeled to him and asked him, Good master, what shall I do that I may inherit eternal life? And Jesus said unto him, thou knowest the commandments,

---

1. Luke 14:33

do not commit adultery, do not kill, do not steal, do not bear false witness, defraud not, honor thy father and mother.

And he answered and said unto him. Master, all these have I observed from my youth.

Then Jesus beholding him, loved him, and said unto him, one thing thou lackest; go thy way and sell whatsoever thou hast and give to the poor, and thou shalt have treasure in heaven, and take up thy cross and follow me.

And he was sad at that saying and went away grieved for he had great possessions.[2]

(In St. Matthew it says, "If thou wilt be perfect, go and sell...")[3]

Some have reasoned that from the Lord's use of, "If thou wilt be perfect," that this was a condition of some high, uncommon perfection which most Christians were not expected to aspire after. But the weakness of this argument soon appears when one considers that the young man's question plainly showed what perfection it was that he aimed at. He only asked what he should do that he might inherit eternal life. It was in answer to this question that our Lord told him that though he had kept the commandments, yet he lacked one thing.

When our Savior says, "If thou wilt be perfect," it is the same thing as when He said if you will not be lacking in one thing, you must not only keep the commandments, "but sell all that thou hast and give to the poor." This is not an uncommon height of perfection, but a condition of being a Christian and securing an inheritance of eternal life.

This truth is underlined by our Lord's general remark upon it, "How hardly shall they that have riches enter into the kingdom of God. It is easier for a camel to go through the eye of a needle, than for a rich man to enter into the kingdom of God."[4]

How could it be said of rich men that they can hardly and with difficulty enter into the kingdom of God if they were not held to the same standard as the rich young ruler? The same self-renunciation is required of all men.

The disciples plainly understood the Lord's meaning, for they said, "Who then can be saved?"[5] Our Savior's answer shows that He did not think they misunderstood Him, for He answers that with God

2. Mark 10:17-22   3. Matthew 19:21   4. Mark 10:25   5. Mark 10:26

all things are possible, implying that it was possible for the grace of God to work this great change in the hearts of men.

Those who will still fancy that this command related only to this young man ought to observe that he was very virtuous and so eager for eternal life that he ran to our Lord and put the question to him upon his knees, and for these things our Savior loved him.

Can it be imagined that Jesus would make salvation more difficult for one so disposed than for others? Would He make him lacking in one thing which other men might lack in all ages without hindering their salvation? Would He send him away sorrowful on account of such terms as are no longer applicable to the Christian world?

As this cannot be supposed, we must aver that our Savior required nothing of that young man that was unusual, or demanded anything that was not for the excellency of the gospel and always to be required of all Christians. It is as easy to conceive our Lord's allowing less restitution and repentance in some sinners than in others as that He should make more denial of the world, more affection for heaven necessary for some than for others.

It is undeniable that an obedience to this doctrine revealed an excellent standard. It extolled the most noble virtues of the soul. It judged rightly of the vanity of earthly riches and the right value of heavenly treasures, as well as the proper stance of true devotion to God.

If this standard is so excellent, why is it not viewed in that light today? Has heaven or earth undergone a change? Is the world now more worth our notice or heavenly treasure of less value than in our Lord's time?

The matter comes to this: either we must say that Christ did not make a reasonable proposal to the young man, or that what He required of him was not sufficiently excellent in itself and advantageous to him, or we must allow that the same proposal is as reasonable for us to accept now as it was in the first ages of the Church.

We must observe, too, that if the reasons which pressed this duty upon the young man recommend it equally to us and if we neglect it, we are equally as unreasonable as he who went away sorrowfully.

Let those who are startled at this doctrine and think it unnecessary now deal faithfully with their own hearts and ask themselves whether they should not have the same dislike of it had they lived in our Savior's days, or whether they can find any reason why they should have been so spiritual and heavenly then and not now.

If this selling all, this renunciation of worldly wealth was not required for the excellence and spirit of Christianity, it will be hard to show a reason why such voluntary self-denial and renunciation of one's own enjoyments, such persecution of one's self should be required at a time when Christianity exposed its members to such uncommon hatred and persecution from other people.

Then it must be admitted that it is still the same necessary duty and is now as much the proper behavior of those who are the sons of God as it ever was. Christianity is that same spiritual, heavenly state as it was then. It has suffered no alteration.

XII.
The Priceless Pearl

Anyone who is at all acquainted with the Scripture must observe that the doctrine of renouncing the world is the most common and oft-repeated subject of our Lord's heavenly instructions.

A certain man said unto him, Lord I will follow thee whithersoever thou goest, And Jesus said unto him, Foxes have holes, and birds of the air have nests, but the Son of Man hath not where to lay his head.
Another also said, "Lord, I will follow thee, but let me first go bid them farewell that are at home at my house."
And Jesus said unto him, "No man having put his hand to the plough, and looking back is fit for the kingdom of God.[1]

This passage is similar to that spoken to the rich young man and

1. Luke 9:57-58

directly teaches the same renunciation of the world as the first principle and essence of Christianity. This doctrine is urged upon us by various ways and every art of teaching.

"The kingdom of heaven," said our Lord, "is like unto a merchant seeking goodly pearls who, when he had found one pearl of great price, went and sold all that he had and bought it."[2] This parable needs little interpretation. It is plain and strong and presses home the advice that our Lord gave to the rich young man.

When it says that the kingdom of God is "a pearl of great price," it evidently means that a great deal is to be given for it, and when it says that the merchant went and sold all that he had and bought it, it teaches us that it cannot be bought at any less price.

This parable does not suggest that the merchant went to trading again after he had sold all and bought this pearl. He was content with this and did not want any other riches.

The peaceful, pleasurable enjoyment of riches is everywhere condemned by our Savior. "Woe unto you that are full, for ye shall hunger; woe unto you that laugh now, for ye shall weep and mourn."[3]

If we can think for all this that the joys of prosperity and gay pleasures of plenty are allowed enjoyments of Christians, we must have done wondering at the blindness and hardness of the Jews' hearts.

"Woe unto you that are rich, for ye have received your consolation!"[4] This same doctrine is pressed upon us by a remarkable parable which is so plain that one would think that every Christian who has heard it would be afraid of everything that looked like self-indulgence:

There was a certain rich man who was clothed in purple and fine linen and fared sumptuously every day.
And there was a certain beggar named Lazarus who was laid at his gate full of sores and desiring to be fed with the crumbs which fell from the rich man's table; moreover, the dogs came and licked his sores.
It came to pass that the beggar died and was carried by the angels into Abraham's bosom. The rich man also died and

---

2. Matthew 13:45-46   3. Luke 6:25   4. Luke 6:24

was buried, and in hell he lifted up his eyes being in torments and seeth Abraham afar off and Lazarus in his bosom.[5]

This parable teaches again the same truth that was held before the rich young ruler to sell all that he had. It is the bare pleasurable enjoyment, the living in the usual delights of a great fortune that is condemned. No injustice, no villainies or extortions are laid to his charge. It is only a life of splendor and indulgence that leaves him in hell.

This is underscored by what Abraham answered, "Son, remember that thou in thy life-time receivedst thy good things. This is alleged as the sole reason of his being in torments. Nothing is mentioned of Lazarus but his low and afflicted state, and then it is "he is comforted and thou art tormented."[6]

Can anything show us more plainly the impossibility of enjoying mammon while we live and God when we die? Does not this manifestly teach us that same renunciation of worldly enjoyments as if we had been expressly required to part with all that we have? If a life of splendor and pleasure and sensual gratification is the portion of those who choose to enjoy it, if it exposes us to so much woe and wrath hereafter, well might our Lord tell the rich man that he lacked one thing, that he was to sell all that he had and give to the poor.

If, therefore, time has not worn away this parable's meaning, it contains a doctrine that concerns all rich men. It calls as loudly for a renunciation of all worldly indulgences for all men as it did for the rich young man. There is no advantage gained by considering our Lord's command as a particular charge to a particular young man.

If we will here appropriate this parable to a special person, we should as reasonably maintain that the hell in which he was tormented was made only for him and is a state which no one else has any occasion to fear.

We must, therefore, believe that Christianity is still that same opposite state to the world that it was in our Savior's days, that He speaks to us the same language that He spoke to the young man in the gospel, that if we will not hear His voice but indulge ourselves in the proud sensual delights of riches and grandeur, to us belongs that dreadful threatening, "Woe unto you that are rich, for ye have received your consolation."[7]

I know it has been said that all we are taught by the command given to the young man to "sell all" is that whenever we cannot keep our possessions without violating some essential duty of a Christian, then, and not till then, need we think we are called upon by Christ to quit all and follow Him.

XIII.
The Eye of the Needle

I have shown that the requirement made of the young man was no particular duty, but that which the Savior placed upon all. I have shown that the same doctrine is taught generally by comparing the kingdom of God to one pearl of great price which the merchant could buy for no less a price than by selling all that he had. The parable of the rich man in torments tells graphically of the result of living in the state and pleasures of a fortune.

Now if all that is taught by the case of the young man in the gospel is that we are to part with our enjoyments and possessions when we cannot keep them without renouncing some great truth of our religion, how is a good Christian to be assured that this is a safe and just interpretation? How shall we know that there is no danger in following it? Such interpretation is not the open, direct sense of the words. The text says *sell all* that you have. It does not say, "Ye need not sell yet" nor "ye need not sell at all, but keep them and enjoy them till such a time as you cannot keep them without denying the faith."

Such an interpretation is as contrary to many other parts of the

---

7. Luke 6:24

Scripture as to this text. It is contrary to the spirit of Christianity, and is only brought in to soften the rigors of religion, that people may with quiet consciences enjoy the pleasures of plenty and those who want it to spend their time in the ways and means of acquiring it.

If there is not an entire change in the way to heaven, if the once strait gate is not now a wide and open passage to all full, fat, and stately Christians, if there is still any meaning in the words, "Blessed are the poor in spirit, for theirs is the kingdom of heaven,"[1] the serious Christian may as well doubt this allowance of enjoying the pleasures and plenty of possessions until persecution drives him out of it—as if he were told that he need not resist the devil till such a time he tempted him to deny the faith or give up some truth of his religion.

When our Savior gave this commandment to the young man and afterwards observed upon his refusal that it was easier for a camel to go through the eye of a needle than for a rich man to enter into the kingdom of God, the apostles took that command to signify the common conditions of entering into Christianity and immediately declared that they had left all and followed Him.

Our Lord answered them in such a manner as showed that the doctrine then delivered related to all mankind in the same sense and had nothing particular in it that related to one man or to one age of the Church more than another: "Verily, I say unto you, there is no man that hath left house or brethren or sisters or father or mother or wife or children or lands for my sake, or the gospel's, but he shall have a hundredfold now in this present time . . . and in the world to come eternal life."[2]

Let us now suppose it was barely lawful to enjoy our worldly goods. Is there any profit in it? Is this a state of any merit? If it is not a sin, it is at best a losing of our time. On the other hand, if we come up to the doctrine of the text, if we part with our worldly gratifications for the sake of Christ, we are assured we shall receive a hundredfold and in the world to come eternal life.

If such persons as these are to be blessed in this life and rewarded in the next, it is certain that they who are not such persons will not be so doubly blessed both in this life and in that which is to come. And

---

1. Matthew 5:3   2. Mark 10:29-30

who will follow an interpretation that savors of the wisdom of this world and leads away from the perfection of the soul?

Our Savior and His apostles, both in doctrine and practice, are on the side of renouncing the enjoyment of riches, and who is he who dares preach a worldly peace and indulgence without either a text or a precedent from Scripture and such a peace as leads men from high rewards both in this life and that which is to come?

When Jesus told Peter of His sufferings, Peter "took him and began to rebuke him, saying, Be it far from thee, Lord; this shall not be unto thee. But he turned and said unto Peter, Get thee behind me, Satan, thou art an offence unto me, for thou savorest not the things that be of God, but those that be of men!"[3]

An interpretation that runs counter to the plain, open sense of these words and leads away from those great rewards that belong to it, that is not supported by doctrine or practices of the first Christians and is contrary to the heavenly spirit of our religion is not to be admitted. It does not lead to Christian perfection any more than the nonbelief of an honest heathen.

I know many will ask whether all Christians are obliged to sell their estates and give to the poor in order to inherit eternal life. The absurdity of such a thing and the disorder it would occasion will be thought sufficient to expose and confute such a doctrine.

The absurdity of this teaching in the eyes of the world is far from being any objection against it, since we are assured by God Himself that the wisdom of this world is foolishness with God, and that the spirit of Christianity and the spirit of the world are as contrary to one another as the kingdom of light and the kingdom of darkness.

What can be more contrary to worldly greatness and wisdom than the doctrine of the cross?

We must disregard the maxims and wisdom of this world and not form our judgments of Christian virtues by them, since by them patience and meekness may be reckoned shameful and revenge and murder as instances of honor.

---

3. Matthew 16:22,23

XIV.
Selling "All"

I now answer directly the question whether Christians are asked literally to sell their possessions and give to the poor in order to have treasure in heaven.

When the Lord bade the young man to "sell all," He required him to renounce the self-enjoyment of his estate—to live no longer in the gratifications of his plenty, but to offer it all to God in works of charity and relief of others.

Now the *selling all* is only a circumstance of parting with the *enjoyment* of riches and turning to these objects and actions as are worthy in the sight of God.

If our Lord had told sinners that they must repent in sackcloth and ashes, I should have thought that sackcloth and ashes were only mentioned as a particular way of expressing a general duty and that the circumstance of sackcloth and ashes might be omitted. But the thing intended, the degree of humiliation and sorrow, was always to be performed in the same degree.

I take it to be the same in the case before us. It is not necessary that a man should literally *sell all* that he has because that was the expression used to the young man. But it is necessary that he comply with the thing signified, and practice all that disregard of the world and heavenly affection which is there taught.

He sufficiently sells all who parts with the self-enjoyment of it and makes it the support of those that need it. This seems to me to be the true and plain meaning of the passage. The words *sell all* are only used as a form of speech as a general way of expressing the parting with the enjoyment of possessions, as sackcloth and ashes were a general way of expressing repentance.

A person who was to give away his goods would surely comply with the doctrine of the text that shows it is the *thing* signified and not the particular *manner* of doing it that is required. Yet it is the keeping to this literal sense of the words, as if the selling all was the particular thing enjoined, that has taught people to excuse themselves from the real teaching.

There was some pretense to think that so particular an action as the selling all could only relate to him to whom it was enjoined. But if men would consider that this selling all is only a circumstance of repentance, and that the thing required is heavenly affection and devotion to God, they would find themselves as much concerned with that doctrine as any other taught in Scripture.

When the Lord spoke of the Good Samaritan's charity and said to the man, "Go and do thou likewise,"[1] he is not exhorted to stay for an opportunity of doing the same action, but to do the same thing which was implied by that action.

Taking, therefore, the words in this plain sense as an exhortation to such a degree of heavenly affection and disclaiming all self-enjoyment of riches, and not as to any particular action of selling all, one must affirm that they equally apply to all rich men to the end of the world as to the young man to whom they were spoken.

As he was called to that spirit because it was a right spirit for a Christian, a proper instance of faith and hope and devotion to God and a right way of using the things of this world, how can it be thought that the same attitude is not equally right in every rich man now? Or how can it be thought that the rich men of this age are not equally obliged to act conformably to the spirit of religion now as well as in the days of Christ?

Are not humility and meekness to be practiced in the same fullness that they were in our Savior's time? If they are, it will be impossible to show why any other virtues should admit of any abatement. Or can anyone show a better instance of humility and meekness than in departing from the splendid enjoyments of his fortune to make it the support and relief of poor and distressed people?[2]

---

1. Luke 10:37
2. Law gave food and clothing regularly to the needy of King's Cliffe, illustrating the principle taught here that giving to the poor portrays self-denial of riches.

It must be affirmed that we are as much obliged to labor after the same degrees of faith, hope, heavenly affection, and disregard of the world as after the same degrees of humility, charity, and repentance that were ever required of any Christians.

Let it also be considered that the command to sell all is only particular in the expression, but the thing required is the general temper of Christianity as is expressed by being dead to the world, by having our conversation in heaven, by being born of God and having overcome the world. These expressions have no proper meaning if they don't imply all that heavenly affection and disregard of riches to which our Lord exhorted the young man.

XV.
The Unchanging Cost of Discipleship

"God forbid," said St. Paul, "that I should glory save in the cross of our Lord Jesus Christ, by whom the world is crucified unto me and I unto the world."[1]

I desire to know why any Christian should think it less dreadful not to be crucified and dead to the world than St. Paul thought it? Is not the spirit which the Apostle shows here as much to be aspired after as in any other part of Scripture? Or can they be said to have the spirit of Christ who are directed by a spirit contrary to that of the Apostle? Yet the Scripture says expressly that "if any man have not the Spirit of Christ, he is none of His."[2]

This renunciation of the world, which is thought too great an extreme to be taken from the command to the young man in the gospel, is at the very heart of Christianity. It is indeed the natural soil, the proper stock from whence all the graces of a Christian naturally grow forth; it is a disposition most necessary and most productive of virtue.

---

1. Galatians 6:14   2. Romans 8:9

Let us suppose that rich men are now enjoying their riches and taking all the common delights of plenty, that they are projecting and contriving scenes of pleasure and spending their money lavishly.

Let it be imagined that we saw the holy Jesus, who had not where to lay His head, with His twelve disciples who had left all to follow Him. Let us imagine that we heard Him call all the world to take up the cross and follow Him, promising a treasure in heaven to those who would quit all for His sake, rejecting all who would not comply with such terms and pronouncing woe and eternal death upon all who lived in pomp and worldly delights. Let us imagine that we heard Him commanding His disciples to take no thought of what they should eat or drink or with what they should be clothed, saying that "after all these things the Gentiles seek."[3]

Let it be further imagined that we saw the first Christians taking up the cross, renouncing the world, and counting all but dung that they might gain Christ. Let the imagination determine whether it is possible for two sorts of men to be true disciples of the same Lord.

Let us suppose that a rich man was to make this kind of prayer to God: "O Lord, I, thy sinful creature, who am born again to a lively hope of glory in Jesus Christ, beg of thee to grant me a thousand times more riches than I need that I may be able to gratify myself and my family in the delights of eating and drinking and a state of grandeur. Grant that as the little span of life wears out, I may still abound more and more in wealth and that I may perceive all the best and surest ways of growing richer than my neighbors . . . ."

There is no one, I believe, who would not be ashamed to make this kind of prayer to God. However, all who have not truly overcome the world are guilty of the spirit of such a prayer.

As we live, so we really pray, for as Christ says, "Where your treasure is, there will your heart be also."[4] As the manner of our life is, so is our heart; it is continually praying what our life is acting, though not in any express form of words.

Dare we approach God with such a spirit? How dare we then think of approaching Him with such a life? Need we any other conviction that this manner of life is contrary to the spirit of Christian-

---

3. Matthew 6:32   4. Matthew 6:21

ity and that the praying of it in Christ's name comes near to blasphemy?

We may indeed do several innocent things which, on account of their littleness, do not adversely affect our devotions. But if the main actions of our life are not such as we may justly beg the assistance of God's Holy Spirit in the performance of them, we may be assured that such actions make our lives as unholy as wrong petitions.

I think it is sufficiently plain that the present disciples of Jesus Christ have no more to do with worldly enjoyments than those whom He chose while He was upon earth, and that He expects as much devotion to God and heavenly affection from us as from any that He conversed with.

XVI.
No Double Standard
for Rich and Poor

I know it will be asked, "Where can be the impiety of getting and enjoying houses and lands and other earthly possessions? Is it not honorable and a matter of just praise to provide property and other goods for one's family? And what are people of noble birth and fortune to do if they are not to live lives suitable to their station in life?"

The doctrine set before us is not mine; hence I do not have to defend it against such questions as these. The same people may ask why the little span of life is made a state of trial and probation, in which men of all conditions are to "work out [their] salvation with fear and trembling."[1] He who thinks it lawful and creditable to make it the care and design of his life to heap up possessions is too blind to be convinced by arguments. He may with as much re-

1. Philippians 2:12

‎

gard to Scripture say that it is lawful to swear falsely when he knows he is forbidden so to do.

Our Lord says, "Labor not for the meat that perisheth, but for that meat which endureth unto everlasting life."[2] He commands us not to lay up for ourselves treasures on earth; He assures us that we cannot serve God and mammon.

These words have no meaning if it is still lawful for Christians to heap up treasures and to labor for great possessions for the enrichment of their families.

I don't question but that the rich young man in the gospel, who had kept the commandments of God from his youth, could have made a very good apology for himself and have shown how reasonable and innocent it was for so good and so young a man to enjoy earthly goods.

The rich man in torments could have alleged how much good he did with his fortune, how many trades he encouraged by his purple and fine linen and faring sumptuously every day, and how he served society by spending his money freely.

The Apostle says, "Having food and raiment, let us be therewith content, that they who will be rich fall into a temptation and a snare, and into many foolish and hurtful lusts which drown men in destruction and perdition."[3]

We may pretend, notwithstanding what the writer says of a "snare" and a "temptation" and foolish "lusts," that we can pursue the means and desire the happiness of riches without any danger to our virtue. If so, we are as prudent as those Christians who think they can secure their virtue without watching and prayer, though our Savior said, "Watch and pray that ye enter not into temptation."[4]

If we will not be so humble and teachable as to conform to Scripture in the simplicity and plainness of its doctrines, there will be no end of our errors, but we will be in as much darkness as where the light of Scripture never appeared.

The rich man in the gospel was a *ruler,* a *young* man, and a *good* man. If there are any among us that are neither young nor good, it can hardly be thought that they have less to do to inherit eternal life than

---

2. John 6:27   3. I Timothy 6:8-9   4. Matthew 26:41

the young man in the gospel.

The gospel has made no provision for dignity of birth or difference in fortune, but has appointed the same strait gate as the common passage for all persons to enter into glory.

The distinctions of civil life have their use and are in some degree necessary, but if anyone thinks he may be less devoted to God, less afraid of the corruptions of pleasure and the vanities of pride because he was born of one family rather than another, he is as much mistaken as he who fancies he has a right to steal because he was born of a father who was poor.

Why may not poor people give themselves to discontent, to impatience and repining? Is it not because Christianity requires the same virtues in all states of life? Is it not because the rewards of religion are sufficient to make us thankful in every condition? Who does not see that the same reasons equally condemn the gratifications, the sensual indulgences of the rich as the discontents and repinings of the poor?

Hence, a great man taking his swing in worldly pleasures in the various gratifications which plenty can furnish is as good a Christian as the poor man who resigns himself to discontent and spends his time and spirits in restless complaints and repinings.

If the joys of religion and our hopes in Christ are sufficient to make us rejoice in tribulation and be thankful to God in the hardships of poverty, surely the same hopes in Christ must be equally sufficient to make us forbear the luxury and softness and all other pleasures of imaginary greatness.

If, therefore, the rich or great men can find a course of pleasure that supports no wrong turn of mind, a luxury and indulgence which won't gratify sensual delights, or entertainments which indulge no vain and weak passions; if they find self-enjoyments of their riches that show they love God with all their strength and their neighbors as themselves; if they can find instances of splendor and greatness that gratify neither the "lust of the flesh, the lust of the eyes, nor the pride of life," religion has no command against such enjoyments.

Let it be remembered, that if any distinctions of life make men forget that sin is their only baseness and holiness their only honor, if any condition makes them less disposed to imitate the low, humble estate of their suffering Master, or to forget that they are to return to

God by humiliation, repentance, and self-denial, instead of being of any real advantage, it is their curse, their snare and destruction.

Had there been any other lawful way of employing our wealth than in the assistance of the poor, our Lord would not have confined the rich young man to that *one* way of employing all that he had. If there were no sin in pampering ourselves with our riches, our Savior would not have said, "Woe unto you that are rich, for ye have received your consolation."[5] Had a delight in the greatness and splendor of this life been an innocent delight for people of birth and fortune, He would never have said, "Blessed are the poor in spirit, for theirs is the kingdom of heaven."[6] Had worldly mirth and splendor been any part of the happiness of Christians. He would not have said, "Blessed are they that mourn, for they shall be comforted."[7]

Thus, it appears from almost every part of Scripture that a renunciation of the world and worldly enjoyments, either of pleasure or pride, is the necessary attitude of all Christians of every state and condition.

I know it will still be objected that the different states of life are indifferent in themselves and are made good or evil by the attitudes of the people who enjoy them; a man is not necessarily vain because he lives in a low estate.

It is granted that a man in a low estate may be very vain and proud because he is in such a state by circumstances and is restless and uneasy until he can raise himself out of it. If the same can be said of any man who lives in splendor, that he is in it by force of circumstance and is restless and uneasy until he can lay all aside and live in a humble and lowly state, it may be granted that such a man, though in the height of splendor, may be as humble as another who lives in starving circumstances may be proud.

But nothing can be more false than to conclude that because a man may be in a low estate without having lowliness of mind, that, therefore, another may live in all height of grandeur without having any height or vanity of mind.

Again, who does not know that a man may give all his goods to feed the poor and yet want charity? But will anyone therefore con-

5. Luke 6:24   6. Matthew 5:3   7. Matthew 5:4

clude that another may keep all his goods to himself and yet have charity? It is as well argued to say that because a man has nothing to spend, he may yet be proud; though another may lay out his estate in vain expenses, he may yet have true humility of mind.

A man is humble, not for what he has already done, but because it is his continual disposition to oppose and reject every temptation to pride. Charity is a continual struggle with the contrary qualities of self-love and envy. Virtue is a progressive quality of mind that is always laboring to preserve itself.

Those who suppose that they may be so complete in the virtue of humility that they may be truly humble in the enjoyments of splendor and vanity do not consider that humility is never finished, and that it ceases to exist when it ceases to oppose and reject every appearance of pride.

This is the true state of every virtue: resisting and opposing all the temptations to the contrary vice.

To suppose, therefore, a man so truly humble that he may live in all appearances of pride and vanity is as absurd as to suppose a man so inwardly sober that he need refuse no strong drink, so inwardly charitable that he need not avoid quarrels, or so holy that he need not resist temptations to sin.

The necessity of renouncing the world in whatever condition of life we are, besides what appears from particular commands, may be proved from those great degrees of holiness that Christianity requires.

XVII.
Finding True Happiness

Christians are to love God with all their hearts, with all their souls, with all their minds, and with all their strength, and their neighbors as themselves.[1] It is impossible in the nature of things that we should practice any of these duties in any Christian sense unless we are born of God as to have "overcome the world."

A man who has his head and his heart taken up with worldly concerns can no more love God with all his soul and with all his strength than a man who will have his eyes on the ground can be looking towards heaven with all the strength of his sight.

If we are to love God with all our heart and with all our soul, it is absolutely necessary that we be first persuaded that to have no happiness but in Him alone and that we are capable of no other good but what arises from our enjoyment of the divine nature.

We may be assured that we never believe this truth until we resign or renounce all pretensions to any other happiness. For to desire the happiness of riches at the same time that we know all happiness is in God is as impossible as to desire the happiness of sickness when we are sure that no bodily state is happy but that of health.

We are as much obliged to renounce the world with all our heart and strength as we are to love God with all our heart and strength. It is as impossible to do one without the other as to exert all our strength in two different ways at the same time.

It is also certain that we unavoidably love everything in proportion as it appears to our happiness. If it appears to be half our happiness, it will necessarily have half the strength of our love, and if it appears to be all our happiness, we shall naturally love it with all our strength.

The Christian religion, therefore, which requires the whole strength of our nature to aspire after God, lays this just foundation of our performing this duty by commanding us to renounce the happiness of the world, knowing it is impossible to have two happinesses and but one love.

Let anyone deal faithfully with himself—consult his own experience, his inner feelings—and consider whether when his soul is taken up with the enjoyments of this life, he feels that his soul is loving God with all its force and strength. Let any man say that he feels this strong tendency of his soul towards God while it tends towards

---

1. Matthew 22:37,39

earthly goods, and I may venture to depart from all that I have said.

Nothing can be more plain than this: if we are to fill our souls with a new love, we must empty it of all other affections.

The love of God, as I have said of every other virtue, is never in any complete state, but is to preserve and improve itself by a continual opposition and resistance of other affections. It is as necessary to renounce continually the world and all its objects of our affections in order to form the love of God in our hearts as it is to renounce and resist all motives of self-love and envy to beget the habit of charity. A man may as well pretend that little envies are consistent with true charity as that little desires after the vanities of the world are consistent with an entire love of God with all our hearts.

It may be said that though this appears to be true from reason, yet it is a love suited more to angels than to man. I answer, it is what God has required. The same objection may be made against all other Christian virtues, for they are all required in a perfect degree.

If it is a degree of affection hardly attainable, this underscores the doctrine I have delivered and shows the absolute necessity of having no extra distractions from the world. If it is so hard to raise the soul to this degree of love, surely it must be unwise to add to the difficulty by foolish and contrary affections.

If this is the proper love of angels, this proves that it is a proper love for us who are taught by God to pray that His will may be done on earth as it is in heaven. At least, if this is the love of angels, it shows us that we are to imitate it as far as our nature will allow, and to stop at no degrees short of it except such as we cannot possibly reach.

As surely, therefore, as this is the love of angels, as surely are we called to an angelic state of life with God, so surely are we obliged to lay aside every hindrance, to part with every enjoyment that may stop or retard the soul in its rise and affection towards God.

The love of enemies is said to be a love that becomes the perfection of God. But we see that we are so far from being excused from this manner of love because it is divine and suits the nature of God, that we are for that reason expressly called to it that we may be "children of [our] Father which is in heaven."[2]

2. Matthew 5:45

If, therefore, we are called to that spirit of love which becomes the perfection of God, surely the manner of angelic love is not too high for us to aspire after.

All we are to learn from this is that a renunciation of the world is necessary, that this holy love cannot be attained unless we only use the world so far as our needs dictate and think of no happiness but what is prepared for us at the right hand of God.

This entire love of God is as possible as the attainment of several other duties which are still the rules of behavior we are to aspire after in the utmost perfection.

The sincere love of our enemies is perhaps of all other virtues the hardest to acquire, and the motions of envy and spite the most difficult to lay aside. Yet without it we are not qualified to say the Lord's Prayer. We see examples of this love of God in the first followers of our Lord, and though we may not work all the miracles they did, we may arrive at their personal holiness if we would be so humble as to imitate their examples. The early disciples took Christ at His word, but we take upon us to reason about the innocence of wealth and stately enjoyments, and so possess everything but the spirit of our religion.

It is sometimes said that the affections depend much upon the physical constitution. Notwithstanding the differences in constitution, all people are affected by what they reckon as their happiness. If they are not full of a desire for God, it is because they are full of, or at least engaged with, another happiness. It is not any slowness of spirits, but a variety of enjoyments that have taken hold of their hearts and rendered them insensible of that happiness that is to be found in God.

When any man has followed the counsels of our Master, when he has renounced the world, rejected the flattering appearances of worldly happiness, emptied himself of all idle affections, and practiced all the means of fixing his heart upon God alone, he may be pardoned if he still wants such warmth of affection as so great a good might justly raise. But until all this is done, we may as vainly appeal to our constitutions, tempers, and infirmities as the unprofitable servant appealed to the hardness of his master and hid his talent in the earth.

If we know that loving God with all our heart and soul is so opposed to the tempers and infirmities of our nature, why do we not remove every hindrance, renounce every vain affection, and with double diligence practice all means of forming this divine temper? For this we may be assured: seeking happiness in the enjoyments of wealth is as contrary to the entire love of God as wrapping up the talent in a napkin is contrary to improving it.

He who has renounced the world as having nothing in it that can render him happy will find his heart at liberty to aspire to God in the highest degrees of love and desire.

Until we do thus renounce the world, we are strangers to the spirit of piety; we do but act the part of religion and are no more affected with those devotions which are put into our mouths than an actor upon the stage is angry at himself when he speaks an angry speech.

Religion is only what it should be when its happiness has entered into our souls and filled our hearts with its proper spirit, when it is the settled object of our minds and governs and affects us as worldly men are affected with that happiness which governs their actions.

The ambitious man naturally rejoices at everything that leads to his greatness and as naturally grieves at such accidents that oppose it. Good Christians that are so wise as to aim at one happiness will as naturally be affected in this manner.

It is, therefore, as necessary to renounce all the satisfactions of riches and fortune and place our sole happiness in God as it is necessary to love Him with all our hearts and all our souls, with all our minds and all our strength.

XVIII.
Loving Our Neighbor as Ourselves

Another duty which also proves the necessity of this doctrine is the love of our neighbor: "Thou shalt love thy neighbor as thyself."[1]

Now he who thinks he can perform this duty without taking our Savior's advice of forsaking all to follow Him is as much mistaken as if he imagines he loves his neighbor while heaping up treasure for his self-gratification.

If a man would know what this love for his neighbor implies, let him look impartially into his own heart and see what it is he truly desires and then turn all those same wishes to his neighbor. This will make him feel the just measure of his duty better than any other description.

This will also teach him that this true love of his neighbor is as inconsistent with the love of the world as dueling is inconsistent with meekness and forgiveness of injuries. This love is a quality of mind that suits only such beings as have one common, undivided happiness. This is the state of Christians who have as truly one common happiness as they have one common God.

One common undivided happiness being the only possible foundation for the practice of this benevolence, it is demonstrable that if we seek any other happiness than this, we cannot keep clear of such dispositions as will show that we do not love our neighbor as ourselves.

If our happiness depends upon men, our spirituality will necessarily depend upon men, and we shall love and hate people in

---

1. Matthew 19:19

proportion as they help or hinder us in such happiness.

When we are in this state of happiness, it will be no harder to help our neighbor as ourselves than it is to wish them the enjoyment of the same light or the same common air, for these goods, which may be enjoyed by all, are not the occasions of envy. But while we continue as competitors for the imaginary enjoyments of this life, we lay a foundation for such passions as are directly contrary to the fruits of love.

I take it for granted that when our Savior delivered this doctrine of love, He intended it should be a governing principle of our lives. It concerns us, therefore, as we have any regard to our salvation, to look carefully to ourselves and put ourselves in such a state as we may be capable of performing it. In this state we cannot be until we are content to make no more of this world than to supply our necessities and to wait for *one only* happiness in the enjoyment of God.

If anyone's heart can bear him witness that in thought, word, and deed he treats all men with that love which he bears to himself, it must be one whose heart fervently cries out with the Apostle, "God forbid that I should glory save in the cross of Jesus Christ by which the world is crucified unto the world."[2] Any other glory than this, any other use of the world than being thus crucified to it, is inconsistent with this degree of brotherly love.

For a further proof of this truth, we need only to look into the world and see the spirit that appears among most Christians. We need not go to wicked and loose people; we may go into any virtuous family and we shall find that it has its particular friendships and hatreds, its envyings and evil speakings. All this proceeds from the fact that Christians are busy in attending to their worldly interests, intending only to keep clear of dishonest and scandalous practices.

It is not only cheating and other unlawful practices, but the bare desire of worldly things and placing happiness in them that lays the foundation of these unchristian tempers, that begets certain friendships and enmities and divides Christians into separate factions.

Were there no dishonest persons among us, yet if Christians give themselves up to the happiness and enjoyments of this world, there would be still almost the same want of the loving our neighbors as

---

2. Galatians 6:14

ourselves. Their engaging so far in the world, their false satisfaction in
so many things they ought to renounce, their being too much alive to
the world makes all—even the devout and religious—subject to
tempers contrary to the love of their neighbor.

Why is it that most people find it so easy to love, forgive, and
pray for all men at the hour of their death? Is it not because the
reason for enmity and dislike then ceases? All worldly interests
being at an end, all worldly tempers die away with them.

Let this, therefore, teach us that it is absolutely necessary to die
to the world, if we would live and love like Christians.

XIX.
Dominant Desires

Some have imagined that they only renounce the world as it
ought to be when they retire to a cloister or a monastery, but this
is as unreasonable as to make it necessary to lay aside all use of
clothes to avoid the vanity of dress. As there is a sober and reasonable use of particular things, so there is a sober, reasonable use
of the world to which it is as lawful to conform as it is to eat and
drink.

They only renounce the world as they ought who live in the midst
of it without worldly attachments, who comply with the offices of
human life without complying with the spirit that reigns in the world.

Temperance is required in eating and drinking and in other
compliances or area of this life. We may dress, buy and sell, labor,
provide for ourselves and our families, but as these things are lawful
for the same reason that it is lawful to eat and drink, so are they to be
governed by the same religious strictness that is to govern our eating
and drinking. All variation from this rule is like gluttony and
intemperance and fills our souls with such tempers as are contrary to
the spirit of Christ.

The first step that our desires take us beyond necessary things ranks us as worldlings and raises in our minds all those tempers which disturb the minds of worldly men.

You think yourself very reasonable and conformable to Christianity because you are moderate in your desires. You don't desire a huge estate; you desire only a little finery in your dress and only to have things genteel about you. I answer, if this be your case, you are to be happy that you have but few desires to conquer. But if these desires take hold of you as greater desires have of other people, you are in the state of worldly-mindedness as they are and you are no more dead to the world than they who are the fondest of it.

Consider, also, that what you call moderate desires are as great contrarieties to religion as those which you reckon immoderate, because they hold the heart in the same state of false satisfactions, raise the same vain tempers, and do not suffer the soul to rest wholly upon God. When the spirit of religion is your spirit, when heavenly-mindedness is your temper, when your heart is set upon God, you will have no more taste for the vanity of one sort of life than of another.

The spirit of Christianity is the same spirit that was in Christ when He was upon the earth. If we have reason to think that any pretense would have been severely condemned by Him, we have the same reason to be sure it is as severely condemned by Christianity.

It is not the desire of *great* riches; it is the desire of *riches* and a satisfaction in the pleasures of them that is the snare and temptation, that fills men's minds with foolish and hurtful lusts and keeps them in the same state of worldly folly as those whose desires are greater.

You want to leave fortunes to your children that they may have their share of achievement in the world. Consider, are you doing this upon principles of righteousness as the wisest and best thing you can do for yourself or your children? Can you be said to have chosen the "one thing needful" for yourself or them? Is this showing true kindness toward them?

You love your children and, therefore, you would leave them rich. It is said of our Lord that He loved the young rich man who came to Him and as an act of love, He bade him sell all that he had and give to the poor. What a difference! The love which dwells in you is as contrary to that love which dwelt in Christ as darkness is contrary to light.

Suppose that you succeed in your intentions to leave your children rich. What must you say to them when you are dying? Will you then tell them that you have the same opinion of the greatness and value of riches as you ever had, and that you feel the pleasure of remembering how much thought and care you have taken to get them? Will you tell them that you have provided for their ease, indulgence, and station in the world and that they can now do no better than to eat and drink and take their fill of such enjoyments as riches afford? This would be dying like an atheist.

On the other hand, if you will die like a good Christian, you will not endeavor to fill their minds with such thoughts. Will you not tell them that they will soon be in a state when the world will signify no more to them than it does to you, and that there is a deceitfulness, a vanity, a littleness in the things of this life, which only dying men feel as they ought?

Will you not tell them that all your own failings, irregularities of life, defects in devotion, strengths of passions, and failure in Christian perfection have been owing to wrong opinions of the value of worldly things, and that if you had always seen the world in the same light as now, your life would have been more devoted to God and you would have lived more in all those heavenly affections in which you now desire to die?

Will you not tell them that it is the enjoyment of the world that corrupts the hearts and blinds the minds of all people, and that the only way to know what good there is in devotion, what excellence in piety, what wisdom in holiness, what happiness in heavenly affection, what vanity in this life, and what greatness in eternity, is to die to the world and all worldly dispositions?

If you die in a spirit of piety, if you love them as Christ loved His disciples, your kindness will impel you to exhort them to renounce all self-enjoyments as are contrary to those holy tempers and heavenly affection which you now find to be the only good and happiness of human nature.

XX.
Suffering with Christ

Christianity is a doctrine of the cross that teaches a restoration of mankind to the favor of God by the death and sacrifice of Jesus Christ. This being the foundation of the Christian religion, it shows us that all persons who will act conformably to the nature and reason of Christianity must make themselves suffers for sin.

Indeed it would be strange to suppose that men are redeemed by the sufferings of their Savior as a necessary atonement for sin, and yet sinners are to be excused from sufferings.

"Such a high priest became us," says the Apostle, "who is holy, harmless, undefiled, separate from sinners."[1]

If the holiness of Christ rendered His sacrifice acceptable to God, does this not teach us that we must strive to be holy in order to be acceptable to God? If the sufferings of Christ made God more propitious to sin, must we not as well take this way of suffering to make ourselves fitter objects of divine pardon?[2]

There is, therefore, the same reason for sinners to endeavor to conform to the sufferings as to labor after the holiness of Christ, since they both jointly conspire to render us proper objects of its benefits.

Nor is the sinless state of Christ a better reason for us to avoid and flee from sin than His suffering state is a reason for our renouncing all softness and indulgence in pleasures. Had Christ lacked either holiness or sufferings, His sacrifice had been wanting in an essential part. If, therefore, we think we can be accepted

---

1. Hebrews 7:26
2. Law has been criticized for his emphasis upon works to secure salvation. It is well to note he does not deny any merits of the atonement, but stresses the need for man's volitional cooperation in redemption.

of God by holiness without suffering, we contradict the nature of our religion as much as if we expect to be accepted through sufferings without holiness.

It may be said, in the words of our [Anglican] Liturgy, "Christ having by his one oblation of himself once offered made a full, perfect, and sufficient sacrifice, oblation, and satisfaction for the sins of the whole world." The sacrifice of Christ is full and sufficient as it takes away the necessity of legal sacrifice; it has no need to be repeated; and it fully reconciles God to accept us upon the terms of the new covenant.

There is no occasion to suffer for sin in order to make the sacrifice of Christ more complete or to add a further value to the atonement for sin. Christ is well-said to be our sanctification, our holiness and righteousness as our atonement for sin. Yet we should much mistake the Scripture if we should think that because He is our holiness we need not endeavor to be holy ourselves.

Yet this is as good a conclusion as to imagine that we need not suffer for our sins ourselves because Christ's sufferings are a full atonement for sin, for they are no more a sufficient atonement for sin than Christ is our sufficient holiness. We may as well trust to His holiness without endeavoring to be holy ourselves as to trust to His suffering, the very nature of religion is an undeniable argument that

Let it now be observed, therefore, were that there no precepts or doctrines that expressly called us to a state of self-denial and self-suffering. The very nature of religion is an undeniable argument that the way of suffering is the right and certain way for sinners to find God more propitious to their sin.

He who doubts this must suppose that God required a way of atonement in Jesus Christ that had nothing of atonement in it. That Christ's sufferings have not made all other sufferings for sin needless is plain from the fact that all Christians are still subject to death, for death is a suffering for sin.

Since all Christians are to offer up their bodies at death as a sacrifice or suffering for sin, the teaching is plain that a state of self-denial and suffering is the proper state of this life, for surely it must be proper to make every part of our life suitable to such an end.

When the suffering for sin is over, there will be no death. But so long as death lasts, so long are all beings that are subject to death in a state that requires humiliation and suffering. And they rebel against God who do not make their lives conformable to that mark of divine displeasure which death signifies.

Hence, as the mortality of our condition is a certain proof that our life is in disorder and unacceptable to God, so it is also a proof that we ought to refuse pleasures and satisfactions that are a state of disorder and wait for joy and delights until we are removed to such a state of perfection as God will delight to continue to all eternity.

The Apostle tells us that "flesh and blood cannot inherit the kingdom of God."[3] Must we not, therefore, be very unreasonable if we cast about for mirth in such a condition or give ourselves up to the vain pleasures and indulgences of a flesh and blood which are too corrupt, too unholy to enter the kingdom of God?

The following will show us the excellency and reasonableness of our Savior's doctrine: "He said unto them all, if any man will come after me, let him deny himself, take up his cross daily, and follow me. For whosoever will save his life shall lose it, and whosoever will lose his life for my sake, the same shall save it."[4] Here is a common condition proposed to all who would be Christ's disciples. To show that this applies to all Christians, St. Mark tells us that He called all the people to Him with His disciples—at the same time He gave them the cup of communion.

If it be argued that all Christians are to receive the cup because at the institution of the sacrament it is said, "Drink ye all of this," is it not as good an argument that all Christians are to deny themselves and take up their cross daily because it is delivered in the same manner?

If the Scriptures only called the first disciples of Christ to an external state of sufferings and persecutions from other people, it might with some pretense be supposed only to relate to people when they are in such a state of persecution. But as it calls them to *deny themselves*, to take up their cross daily, it is plain that it calls them to a suffering and self-denial which they are to accept as God's natural course.

---

3. I Corinthians 15:50   4. Luke 9:23,24

If they are called to deny themselves and be subject to voluntary cross-bearing in order to be Christ's disciples, it will be difficult to show that self-denials are not as integral a part of Christianity as baptism and the Lord's Supper. Water baptism is necessary because our Lord has instituted it, and the reason for continuing it is the same as for observing it at first. But still, it is an external rite, or sacrament, which in itself has nothing of holiness or purification of the soul; it has its excellency from the institution of Christ. This cannot be said of sufferings associated with the cross; these have *internal* and *essential* relation to holiness and purification in the present state of man.

I say of the present state of man, though these self-denials or mortifications are proper only to man while he is in this state of corruption, yet they are as truly parts of holiness and as essential virtues as those that will last forever.

Charity to the poor is founded in the necessities and infirmities of this life, but it is as real a degree of holiness and as much to be performed for its own sake as that charity which will never have an end.

If Christ, the Lord of all and Head of the Church, is still making intercession for us at the right hand of God, does not this plainly imply than we are not pleasing to God unless we live in a state of supplication and prayer for ourselves?

If He who had no sin of His own was obliged to undergo such sufferings to make Him an advocate for sin, surely sinners will not presume to sue for their own pardon without putting themselves in the life state of humiliation and suffering. Since the atonement is made by sufferings, it recommends sufferings to sinners as if it had been made a way of prayer for pardon.

Hence, self-denials and sufferings are duties essential to the present state of sin and recommend us to God as holiness and purity recommend us by their own nature and intrinsic fitness; that is, they are good as prayer, humility, and charity are good.

XXI.
Made Perfect Through Suffering

When we shall be removed to a state that is free from sin, self-denial and mortification will then be no part of our duty; but as long as this state of sin lasts, so long does the reason and necessity for self-denial and mortification last. They are as necessary as prayers and devotion and are as truly essential parts of holiness as chastity and humility. Repentance and sorrow for sin are as necessary on their own account as the love of God is necessary for human happiness.

To express our indignation and to inflict punishment on that which displeases God is as reasonable in itself and as much an act of holiness as to love and cherish that which God loves. Hence all our self-denials as punishments of sin, as expressions of sorrow for guilt, and as preventions of temptations, may be considered as so many instances of our love and purity.

While, therefore, we continue in a state of corruption, it is as necessary that we continue in a state of repentance, self-denial, and sorrow as it is necessary to continue our desires and endeavors after purity.

If we consider the reason and fitness of repentance, we see the reason and fitness of self-denial and voluntary sufferings and must acknowledge that these are not less necessary nor less recommended than repentance and sorrow for sin. Though charity and the love of God will never cease and this self-denial will have an end, yet this self-denial during this state of sin is as essential to the holiness of persons in such a state as any other virtue.

If a person were to give himself up to sorrow in a state of happiness, or to unthankfulness though in the midst of mercies, he would act just as unreasonably and as contrary to the nature of things as he who gives himself up to pleasures and indulgences in a state of corruption for sin. Let a Christian ever cease from self-denial, let him ever forbear the mortification of his appetites, at that time he ceases to consider himself as a sinner and behaves himself as though he were then free from guilt and danger of sin.

But as he never is in this state of freedom, if he acts as if he were, he acts as falsely as if he took himself to be an angel.

A man may as well imagine that he prays or gives thanks to God when he only repeats the words of a prayer as that he repents for his sins unless his repentance be a real punishment, a true state of mortification.

We may now observe that this doctrine of self-suffering is founded upon the most important fundamental articles of our faith. If we consider our redemption as an atonement made by suffering, does this not show us the necessity of seeking pardon by a fellowship in the sufferings of Christ? Need we any other argument that there is no state so suitable to a sinner as that of suffering when God has appointed sufferings as the atonement for sin?

Could there be any necessity for our dying to sin if we might lead a life of a contrary nature? Or could we act more contrary to God than by making that life a state of pleasure and indulgence which He has laid under the curse of death? Ought we to indulge a life which God considers too unholy to continue to live?

If we consider that repentance is the chief, the most constant and perpetual duty of a Christian, that our holiness has hardly any other existence than what arises from a perpetual repentance, can it be doubted that mortification and self-denial are essential, perpetual parts of our duty? For to suppose a repentance without the pain of mortification and the punishment of self-denial is as absurd as to suppose a labor after holiness which takes not one step towards it.

Hence, self-denial and mortification are inextricably bound up with repentance, for there is nothing in the nature of repentance that shows it to be a more constant duty or more essential to the Christian life than there is in mortification and self-suffering.

It is very absurd to suppose that Jesus' command to His disciples that they deny themselves and take up their cross daily should mean only the enduring and expecting of sufferings for some and not others.

Let us suppose that Christian churches are full of fine gay people who spend their days in all the pleasures which the spirit of the world can invent. Can it in any sense be said of such that they live in a state of repentance and sorrow for sin? May they not with as much regard to truth be said to live in sackcloth and ashes?

If we will not destroy the whole state of religion, if we will but own it to be a state of trial and probation, we must also allow that self-denial and abstinence from inordinate pleasures are daily essential duties of it, for a life of sorrow for sin and a life of indulgence are inconsistent and necessarily destroy one another as motion puts an end to rest.

Repentance will have no place in heaven because that will be a state of perfection, and for the same reason it ought never to be laid aside on earth because here there is no time when we are not under guilt and subject to the danger of sin.

This does not suppose that we are always to be uttering forms of confessions from our mouths, but it supposes that we are always to live with so much watchfulness as becomes penitent sinners and never do anything but what highly suits a state of repentance.

Whenever we can abate our self-denials without abating our sorrow for sin, when we can find pleasures that neither soften the mind nor make it less fearful of temptation, then, and only then, may we seek our ease. For while repentance is only a lipwork at stated times, it has not had its effect until it has entered into the state and habit of our lives and rendered us as fearful of sin as when we are making our confessions from the heart.

This state of penitence, which alone is suited to a state of corruption and infirmity, can no more exist without constant daily self-denial than we can daily govern our appetites without looking after them.

XXII.
The Happiness of Mourning

Our Lord said, "Blessed are they that mourn, for they shall be comforted."[1] This is another call to self-denial and cessation from worldliness. The blessedness that is here ascribed to mourning must be understood as a state of life and not any transient acts or particular times of mourning, for no single acts are valuable, or rewardable, but as they arise from a state of mind that is constant and habitual.

If it had been said blessed are the charitable, it must have meant blessed are they who live in a state and habit of charity. For the same reason are we to understand that the blessedness which is due to mourning is due only to a state and life of mourning.

"Blessed are they that mourn" shows us that this mourning concerns all men without any distinction of time, so that its excellency and fitness must be founded upon something that is common to all times and all persons.

If this mourning be reasonable and excellent and leads all men to blessedness, it must be founded in the common condition of man. What can this state of mourning be but a godly sorrow founded upon a true sense of the misery of our state—a state of fallen spirits living in sin and vanity and separation from God? What can it be but a ceasing to revel in the false goods and pleasures of this life because they delude and corrupt our hearts, increase our blindness, and remove us farther from God?

What mourning can be blessed but that which mourns at what displeases God, which condemns and rejects what the wisdom of God

---

1. Matthew 5:4

rejects, which loosens us from the vanity of the world, lessens the weight of our corruption, and quickens our aspirings towards perfection? This is not a mourning that shows itself in occasional fits of sorrow or dejection of the mind, but is a regular temper and manner of life.

"Blessed are they that mourn, for they shall be comforted" is the same thing as saying, "Miserable and cursed are they that do not mourn, for they shall not be comforted." Again, "Blessed are the poor in spirit, for theirs is the kingdom of heaven."[2]

Nothing can carry a greater denial and contradiction of all the ways of the world than this doctrine. It not only puts an end to all that we esteem wicked and immoderate desires of worldly satisfaction, but calls us from all worldly satisfactions which in any way fasten the soul to any false goods and make it less ardent after true happiness. As the Christian religion regards only the salvation of our souls and restoring us to a life with God in heaven, it considers everything as ill that keeps us in any state of false enjoyment and nothing as good but what loosens us from the world and makes us less slaves to its vanities. "Blessed are the poor in spirit" because it is a spirit of disengagement and disrelish of the world that puts the soul in a state of liberty and fitness to relish and receive the offers of true happiness.

Let anyone consider how it is possible for a man to be poor in spirit but by renouncing those delights that are high and rich in spirit. A man is high in spirit when his state and dignity give him a pleasure; he is rich in spirit who seeks and delights in the felicities which riches afford. He is, therefore, poor in spirit who mortifies all vain thoughts, rejects every self-pleasure, and avoids and dislikes the empty satisfactions which riches and fortune give.

No one is to reckon himself poor in spirit until he rejects all instances of pride and self-pleasure, until he desires things that are proper to a poverty of spirit as food is proper to hunger or water to thirst.

Every spirit must only be known by the nature of the thing it covets. If we are high-minded, our care will be exercised about high things; if we are lowly in heart, we shall as certainly not only con-

2. Matthew 5:3

descend, but seek after things that are lowly. Let a man, therefore, who would deal faithfully with himself, consider not only whether he is proud, luxurious, indulgent of himself and devoted to pleasures and satisfactions of this life, but let him consider whether he is poor in spirit, whether the things he seeks, the designs he espouses, the happiness he aims at, and the course of his life be such as are really directed by a true poverty of spirit.

This is that self-denial, holy discipline, cross-bearing to which all Christians are called. By thus losing their lives, by ceasing to live the life in accord with this world, they may purchase for themselves endless happiness in another state.

I believe there are very few Christians who do not acknowledge that Christianity is still in some degree a doctrine of the cross. However, they believe this in such a general and loose way that they feel no condemnation of themselves, whatever their lives are, from hearing these doctrines.

XXIII.
Turning the Other Cheek

Another plain and remarkable teaching of self-denial is seen in the following words of our Lord:

> Ye have heard that it hath been said, An eye for an eye and a tooth for a tooth: But I say unto you, That ye resist not evil: but whosoever will smite thee on thy right cheek, turn to him the other also. And if any man will sue thee at law and take away thy coat, let him have thy cloak also. And whosoever shall compel thee to go with him a mile, go with him twain.[1]

Here He instructs us in several instances of self-denial and daily cross-

1. Matthew 5:38-41

bearing which are now the common terms of salvation. We are to deny ourselves in not demanding a tooth for a tooth; we are to take up our cross daily by turning our cheek to the smiter and suffer such ill-usage as we could prevent by resistance. We are to deny ourselves in not defending ourselves by suits at law. We must take up the cross of one injury after another rather than appeal to the contention of a trial. This is sufficiently taught by our being required to expose ourselves to the further loss of our cloak rather than have recourse to law to secure our coat.

The words of this doctrine are so plain that they need little illustration. It is plain, also, that they belong to Christians of all ages. They were doctrines of the cross which were to be perpetual marks of Christ's followers.

"But I say unto you, that ye resist not evil."[2] "Love your enemies, bless them that curse you."[3]

This degree of love which we are to show to our enemies is as much a doctrine of the cross as that of patience, meekness, and submission which we are to show to those who treat us injuriously. These virtues are also necessary to one another. We cannot love God and do good to our enemy unless we are thus patient under sufferings and deny ourselves all instances of anger and uneasiness at them.

It is pretended by some that these passages only forbid our prosecution of *spiteful* and *malicious* suits at law. But such people might as well pretend that the eighth commandment only forbids wanton and spiteful stealing, but allows it when it is done soberly and with no spiteful intention.

Our Lord's words were directed against such a pretense as this. In the case where the man was sued for his coat, he did not consider that it was his own coat or that he entered into the trial to secure his coat. He is not allowed to show contention or anger or injustice or impatience under suffering, but is patiently to permit his coat to be taken from him, though that patience be the means of losing his cloak also.

If Christians will still think that they may defend all their rights and enter into such contentions for them as the laws of the land will

---

2. Matthew 5:39   3. Matthew 5:44

support them in, if they think that they need not bear other injuries but such as courts of law cannot redress, they are as much mistaken as if they imagine they need practice no other charity or worship of God but such as humane laws demand. For Christian meekness, self-denial, and patience under sufferings are no more to be formed by the standard of human laws than our devotion to God.

In these things Jesus Christ is our only lawgiver, and His laws are to be complied with as the certain terms of our salvation.

Notwithstanding that we may be able either by personal power or legal contention to repel injuries, return evil for evil, and demand a tooth for a tooth, yet as disciples of Christ we are to turn our cheek to the smiter and let him that would take away our coat have our cloak also, and be content rather to suffer many injuries than by defending ourselves, raising our passions, embittering our tempers, and destroying that charity which we owe to our neighbor.

This meekness and self-denial is highly suitable to the spirit and temper of Christianity. It is highly suitable to a religion that restores sinners to God by sufferings; it is consistent with such as have forsaken all to follow Christ, to such as be dead and crucified to the world, to such as are to be meek and lowly as Christ; it is suited to such as are commanded to love and do all good to their most violent enemies and who are to love their neighbors as themselves.

Let Christians consider that it is of these doctrines of the cross that our Savior says, "For whosoever shall be ashamed of me and of my words, of him shall the Son of man be ashamed when he shall come in his glory and in his Father's, and of the holy angels."[4] Further, "This is my commandment, That ye love another, as I have loved you."[5]

This love towards mankind knew of no enemies or refused any sufferings, but was a continual laboring for the salvation of all men. If, therefore, we treat any person as our enemy, or fly in the face of those who injure us, we are fallen from that love which is to govern all our actions. Every resistance or contention is a quarrel which begets some degree of spite and ill-will, though they may often be carried on with some show of outward decency.

---

4. Luke 9:26   5. John 15:12

We must, therefore, bear with injuries and wrongs, not because it is difficult to redress them, but because it is difficult, if not impossible, to resist and contend with our adversaries without forfeiting that humility, meekness, and divine love to which we are called. We must suffer with patience because such patience is an exercise of our self-denial that renders us more like our Lord and Master.

We are told of our Lord that though He were a son, yet He learned obedience by the things which He suffered. If He who was a son without sin and full of divine knowledge received instruction from sufferings, surely we who are poor, infirm creatures must want the instruction which is to be learned from them.

To suppose that we can be obedient to God without sufferings is to suppose that we can do our duty without such helps as the Son of God had. Sufferings are, therefore, to be considered among the graces of God which purify our souls, enlighten our minds, and prepare us to perfect holiness in the fear of God.

But how contrary to the spirit of Christ do we act if our sufferings provoke us into methods of retaliation, and instead of teaching us obedience to God, lead us into a state of enmity towards our brethren.

The writer of the book of Hebrews says ". . . for whom are all things, and by whom are all things, in bringing many sons unto glory, to make the captain of their salvation perfect through sufferings."[6] Here we are taught that not only was Christ made perfect through sufferings, but that it was fit He should be made perfect that way as the only way that could bring many sons unto glory.

We see that one end of Christ's sufferings before His being crowned with glory and honor was to teach us that suffering is the way to arrive at glory, and that those who desire to be sons of glory must first be made perfect through sufferings. We mistake the one great design of Christ's sufferings and go out of the road to glory if we do not patiently submit to suffering, if we are not thankful that we suffer with Christ that we may reign with Him.

St. Peter said to some of the Lord's followers, "This is thankworthy if a man for conscience toward God endure grief,

6. Hebrews 2:10

suffering wrongfully. If when ye do well and suffer for it ye take it patiently, this is acceptable with God. For even hereunto were ye called because Christ also suffered for us, leaving us an example, that ye should follow his steps."[7]

Further, sufferings are said by our Lord to promote our happiness and become the basis of real and solid joy: "Blessed are ye, when men shall revile you and persecute you, and shall say all manner of evil against you falsely, for my sake. Rejoice and be exceeding glad: for great is your reward in heaven."[8] Christ does not endeavor to comfort us in this state as if it were a hard or melancholy state which we must bear because it is made easier with patience, or because God is pleased to impose it upon us, but He looks at it in quite another view—not as needing comfort, but as having matter fit for congratulation.

Be the hardships of self-denials what they will, if they make us more like Christ, they have done more for us than all the prosperity in the world can do, and he that defends himself at the expense of any of the qualities of Christ has done himself an injury greater than the worst and most powerful of his enemies can bring on him.

All this is founded upon the reason that there is but one thing needful—the salvation of our souls. It is this that changes the nature of all human things and makes everything good or evil only so far as it promotes or hinders this one end of life. The salvation of the world is the only happiness of the world, and he who has secured his share in that has secured to himself all the joy and gladness that can befall human nature.

---

7. I Peter 2:20-21   8. Matthew 5:11,12a

XXIV.
God and Infinite Reason

Every duty or virtue of the Christian life is founded in truth and reason and is required because of its fitness to be done and not because God has power to command what He pleases.

If we are commanded to be meek and humble, it is because meekness and humility are suitable to the truth of our state, as it is appropriate for every dependent being to be thankful for mercies. If we are bidden to rejoice, it is at something that is truly joyful; if to fear, it is to fear something that is really dreadful.

God is reason and wisdom itself, and He can no more call us to any tempers or duties but those that are strictly reasonable in themselves than He can act against Himself or contradict His own nature. As we can say with assurance that God cannot lie, so we may with the same certainty affirm that He cannot enjoin anything upon rational creatures that is contrary to their nature than He can enjoin them to love things that are not lovely or to hate things that are in their nature not hateful.

When God speaks, we are as sure that infinite Reason speaks as we are sure there is a God. A religion from God has only reasonable commands to reasonable creatures. No demands can be imposed upon us by way of a task or imposition which we might as reasonably be without. God can only will that reasonable creatures should be more reasonable, more perfect, and more like Himself and consequently can enjoin upon us no duties or dispositions of mind that do not tend in these directions. All His commands are for our sakes founded in the necessities of our natures and are only so many instructions to become more happy than we could be without them.

A good man who enjoys the use of his reason is offended at madmen and fools because they act contrary to the reason of things. The madman fancies himself and everything about him to be different from what they are; the fool knows nothing of the value of things, is ridiculous in his choices, and belittles the most useful things in life. A good man, merely through the love of reason, is offended at their conduct and would do all he could to abate the frenzy of the one and the stupidity of the other.

Man in his present state of disorder and ignorance must appear to God both as fool and mad, for every sinner is truly mad when he imagines himself and all things around him to be what they are not; he is a fool as he is ridiculous in his choices and mistakes the value of things.

Now, true religion is our cure. It is God's merciful communication of such rules and disciplines of life as may serve to deliver us from the infatuation and ignorance of our fallen state.

God presses His instructions upon us with terrors and threatenings and makes those virtues which are the natural good and cure of our souls.

Some people are so weak as to wonder why what we call sin should be so odious to God or what it can signify to God whether we are wise or foolish. But let these consider that God is wisdom and reason, and consequently everything that is contrary to reason and wisdom is contrary to His nature, so that a state of sin is contrariety to God. To ask, therefore, why God hates sin is the same thing as to ask why God cannot tell a lie. It is because every deviation from the truth is contrary to His nature, which is truth itself. Hence, every unreasonable act is contrary to His nature, which is reason itself.

It is necessary from the nature of things that every creature be delivered from sin before it can enter into the beatific presence of God, for if God could reward wicked beings and make them happy by the enjoyment of His presence, He would as much cease to act according to the nature of things as if He should punish a being that lived in innocence. To punish innocence and to reward sin are equally contrary to nature and reason.

If some things are so odious in themselves that even the reason of man cannot but abhor them, how much more odious, how much more contrary to the perfection of the divine nature must the folly and madness of sin be.

God is love; yet it is certain that He can only love such things that are lovely. God is goodness, yet He cannot make sinners happy because there is so much contradiction to reason and perfection in making sinners happy as in loving things that are not truly lovely or in hating things that are not truly hateful. This may give us in some measure an idea of the nature of religion and the nature of sin. It will show us that religion is God's gracious method of delivering us from the unreasonableness and corruption of our natures, that by complying with its rules and discipline we may be so altered in our natures, so restored to reason, as to be fit for the rewards of an infinitely wise and perfect Being, that sin is the misery and disorder, the madness and folly of our nature which separate us from God.

Consider the proposition that God loves all things accordingly as they are lovely. Is this not as certain as that God is reason itself? Could He be perfectly reasonable if He did not regard things according to their natures? Must He not hate those things that are truly hateful and love those things so far as they are lovely? To act by any other rule is to act by humor and caprice.

This should teach us that as we are in ourselves, so we are necessarily either odious or acceptable to God. So far as we cease from sin and suffer ourselves to be made wise and reasonable by the wisdom and reason of religion, so far we make ourselves objects of the love of that infinitely perfect Being who necessarily loves beings as they are lovely in nature.

So far as we continue in the madness and folly of sin and neglect the rules of religion which would deliver us from the guilt and slavery of it, so far we make it necessary for that perfect Being to hate us who cannot but hate things accordingly as they are in themselves hateful.

Some people, either through self-love or some confused opinion of God and themselves, are always imagining themselves to be particular favorites of God, imagining all their little successes or blessings in their health and circumstances above other people to be distinguishing marks of God's particular kindness towards them. But such persons must consider that God is reason itself, that He is subject to no particular fondness no more than He is capable of weakness, and that He can no more love them with any special love that is not an act of the highest reason that He can lie or act contrary to the truth. They should realize that afflictions have a much better claim upon God's favor in this life than success: "For whom the Lord loveth He chasteneth . . . ."[1]

As God is reason itself, to be loved by Him and to be approved by the highest reason is the same thing. If he whose life is not conformable to the highest reason imagines that he is particularly beloved by God, he is guilty of the same absurdity as if he believed that God is not the perfection of reason.

As certainly as there is but one God, it is certain there is but one way of making ourselves objects of His love—by conforming and acting according to the highest reason. When our lives are agreeable in this, then are they agreeable to God. In this way we draw near to God by a wisdom that comes from above and revealed to us to make us such reasonable beings as to be fit objects of His eternal love.

A religion from God must be according to the nature of God, requiring no other change of thoughts or actions but those that are conformable to truth and reason. Reasonableness of actions consists in their fitness to be done. There is a reasonableness in being thankful for mercies; also, in rejoicing in things that are joyful.

Humility is nothing else but a right judgment of ourselves and is only so far enjoined as it is suitable to the truth of our state; for to think worse of ourselves than we really are is no more a virtue than to take five to be less than four. On the contrary, he who is proud offends as much against truth and reason and judges as falsely of himself as the madman who fancies himself to be a king.

Consider the reasonableness and necessity of self-denial. If a person were to walk on a rope across some great river and were asked to deny himself the pleasure of walking in silver shoes or looking about at the beauty of the waves or listening to the noise of sailors or fishing by the way, would there be any hardship in such self-denial? Would not such self-denials be as reasonable as commanding him to love things that will do him good or to avoid things that are hurtful?

1. Hebrews 12:6a

"Strait is the gate, and narrow is the way, that leadeth unto life,"[2] said our Lord. If Christians are to walk in a narrow way "that leadeth unto life," the chief business of their lives must be to deny themselves all those things which may either stop or lead them out of the narrow way. If they think that pleasures and indulgences are consistent with their keeping this narrow way, they think as reasonably as the man upon the rope should think that he might safely use silver shoes or stop in his way to catch fish.

This is the foundation of all Christian self-denial. We are born in slavery to sin and are only to be saved by putting off this "old man" and being renewed in holiness and purity of life. The denials of religion are only the necessary means of salvation as they are necessary to lessen the corruption of our nature, destroy our old habits, alter the taste and temper of our minds, and prepare us to relish and aspire after holiness and perfection.

Since our souls are in a state of corruption and our life is a state of probation, in order to alter and remove this corruption it is certain that everything and every way of life which nourishes and increases our corruption is as much to be avoided as those things which beget in us purity and holiness are to be sought after.

A man who wants health avoids practices that produce illness for the same reasons as he who takes medicine for healing. Self-denial is, therefore, as essential to the Christian life as prayer.

The whole of the matter is that Christians are called from a state of disorder, sin, and ignorance to a state of holiness and resemblance of the divine nature. If there are ways that corrupt our minds, support our vanity, increase our blindness, or nourish our sensuality, all these are as necessarily to be avoided as it is necessary to be holy. If there are any denials or mortifications that purify and enlighten the soul, that lessen the power of bodily passions, that raise us to a heavenly affection and make us taste and relish the things of God, these are to be practices as necessarily as to believe in Jesus Christ.

---

2. Matthew 7:14

XXV.
The Nature and Use of Fasting

No Christian who knows anything of the gospel can doubt whether fasting be a common duty of Christianity, since our Lord has placed it along with secret alms and private prayer. "When thou fastest, anoint thy head, and wash thy face, that thou appear not unto men to fast, but to thy Father which is in secret, and thy Father which seeth in secret, shall reward thee openly."[1]

Here the same instructions and the same reasons are given for private fasting as for secret alms and private prayer. As it is manifestly entitled to the same reward, it is put on the same footing as private prayer and is as equally acceptable to God.

Eating and drinking are the common support of life. But as they are the support of a corrupt life, the nourishment of a disordered body that weighs down the soul, whose appetites and dispositions are in a state of enmity with the life and purity of the soul, it is essential that we take care to support the life of the body as not to occasion sickness and death of the soul.

How far our bodies affect our habits may be seen by the difference between sickness and health, youth and old age. These different states of the body alter our whole ways of thinking, owing to different strength and bodily appetites.

What is the reason that a midnight reflection generally goes deeper than a thought at any other time?[2] It is because the peace and tranquillity of the body gives the soul a liberty then of seeing further

---

1. Matthew 6:17,18
2. The belief that a melancholy mood aids moral perception about the nature of man and life was common among the "graveyard school" of writers, including Thomas Gray and Edward Young. Night time was thought to be most conducive to this state of mind.

into things than at any other time. The difference between the same man full and fasting is similar to the man who after a large meal is changed into discomfort and yawnings. He has created a dullness in his soul as well as perverted his taste.

I mention this to show that fasting has a closer relation to all religious tempers than is generally thought, and that indulgent eating dulls the mind towards all things, including religion.

It is the business of religion, then, to put an end to these states of slavery, to deliver blind man from the laws of flesh and blood and give him a wisdom and constancy, a taste and judgment suitable to the reason and wisdom of the laws of God, and to fill our souls with such principles of peace as may give us habits of tranquillity superior to the changeable tempers of our bodies.

Fasting, as it is a denial of bodily indulgence, as it disciplines the body into a state of obedience and contradicts its appetites, is the most constant and universal means of procuring liberty and freedom of the mind. For it is the love of our body and too much care for its enjoyments that makes us too sensitive to its demands. Whatever we nourish and cherish gains our interest and rules us to a marked degree, for every indulgence of the body in eating and drinking is adding to its power and making all our ways of thinking subservient to it.

A man who makes every day a day of full and cheerful meals will by degrees make the happiness of every day depend upon it and consider everything with regard to it. He may decide to go to church or stay at home as it suits with his dinner.

Let such people deal faithfully with themselves and search out their spirit. Can they think they are born again of God, that they have the spirit of Christ who are subject to the pleasures of gluttony? Can they be said to treat their bodies as temples of the Holy Spirit who make them unfit for the holy service of public worship? Can they be said to offer their bodies unto God as a "reasonable, holy, living sacrifice?"[3] Can they be said to love God with all their heart and all their soul, or to have forsaken all to follow Christ who will not so much as forsake half a meal for the sake of divine worship?

---

3. Romans 12:1

The sin of gluttony is the sin of over-eating. Some may think they are only chargeable with gluttony when they eat until they surfeit their bodies. They may also think they are guilty of drunkenness who drink till they have lost their senses. But there is a much surer rule to go by: "Whether ye eat or drink, or whatsoever ye do, do all to the glory of God."[4] All, therefore, in eating and drinking that is not within the bounds of the glory of God, is offered to something outside God's glory, which is to the corruption and sensuality of our own natures and is the sin of intemperance.

I know some people object that fasting is not a universal duty, that it is rather like some particular medicine or remedy that is only necessary for some unusual cases and particular constitutions. To this it may be answered that if by fasting is meant entire abstinence from all food for a certain period of time, in that sense, it is not a universal and constant duty. But it ought to be observed that this is no more the nature of fasting than a certain form of confession of a specific length is the precise nature of repentance.

As repentance does not consist in any stated, fixed degrees of sorrow and pain for sin which is to be the common repentance for all men at all times, so fasting is not any fixed degree of abstinence from all food which is to be the common measure of fasting for all men at all times; it is rather an exercise of abstinence and self-denial as is proper to everyone's particular state.

If we understand fasting in this sense—that it is an abstinence from such food and pleasure of eating as are proper in every state of life to destroy sensuality, lessen the corruption of our natures, and make us relish spiritual enjoyments—it is a constant and universal duty.

As repentance is a universal duty because the reason for it is common to all men, so fasting is necessary to all men because sensuality, fleshly lusts, and the corruption of bodily tempers is the universal corruption of all men.

To those who object that fasting can not be required of all because some people's constitutions will not allow them to eat

---

4. I Corinthians 10:31

enough for their health, it may be pointed out how some people may be so infirm that they cannot attend the public worship of God. However, public worship is a universal duty though some people's poor health may make them incapable of going to it.

Persons of weak and infirm constitutions have often as much necessity of self-denial as others who are healthy. They have the same sensuality to conquer and the same necessity of their measure of abstinence and denial.

It is no fixed degree of sorrow that is the common repentance of all man; it is no particular sum of money that is the common charity of all men; it is no fixed form or length or hour of prayer that is the common devotion of all men. Yet all these are constant and universal duties.

In like manner, though fasting may be subject to all the same variations, yet it is a constant and universal duty.

If a man were to be angry at those who neglect or despise the service of the church as people who know nothing of religion, and then tells you that he himself never goes but on Good Friday and the thirtieth of January, you would say he knew nothing of the value of church-going. For if prayer and repentance and the service of the church were not common acts of devotion and right and necessary ways of worshiping God, they would not be necessary upon Good Friday or any other day.

In like manner, unless fasting was a common and necessary part of religion, something that was always a proper means of applying to God, it would neither be necessary nor acceptable on those particular days. It is not the day that makes the duty necessary, but the day happens to be the proper occasion of exercising a necessary duty.

When some great calamity happens to you, you do well to make it an occasion for exercising great devotion, but if you stay until some other calamity happens before you pray again, or think that prayer is only proper in times of calamity, you know nothing of devotion.

It is the same thing in fasting. Some great occasion may justly call you to it, but if you forbear fasting till such great occasions happen again, or think that fasting is only proper for such public occasions, you know nothing of the nature of fasting.

If one were to say that he never repents but on those public days, he might as easily defend himself as when he says he only fasts at those times. For is there any benefit in fasting on special days? Does it add anything to one's piety and devotion? Does it make repentance and sorrow for sin more real? Does it abate one's passions and put one in a better state of devotion than when he takes his usual meals? If it has something of these effects, why is it only practiced on one or two special days of the year?

It is no fixed degree of sorrow that is the common repentance of all men; it is no particular sum of money that is the common charity of all men; it is no fixed form or length or hour of prayer that is the common devotion of all men. Yet these are common and universal duties. In like manner, though fasting may be subject to all the same variations, yet it is a constant and universal duty.

When the disciples of our Lord could not cast the evil spirit out of a man who was a lunatic, He not only tells them that it was through want of faith, but He also gives them an important instruction in these words: "Howbeit this kind goeth not out but by prayer and fasting."[5] Does this look as if fasting were an occasional thing? It is ranked with prayer as having the common nature, as being equally prevailing with God. Is this not sufficient to teach us that we must think of fasting as we think of prayer—a proper way of devotion and a right method of appealing to God?

If we were to fast without praying, would this not be a way of worship of our own invention? And if we pray and neglect fasting, is it not equally choosing a worship of our own? For He who has taught us the use and advantage of prayer has taught us the same things of fasting; He has joined them together as having the same power with God.

The reason for self-denial and abstinence is constant because we are perpetually united to a body that must be directed into actions consonant with a holy life. This means that one should be temperate in all things, if he is to put on Christ. He must practice the subjection of his body if he is to nurture virtue and lessen the strength of temptation.

---

5. Matthew 17:21

XXVI.
The Measure of Humility

Self-love, pride, vanity, revenge, hypocrisy, and malice are acknowledged as being very gross sins, and indeed they are of the very nature of the devil and as certainly destroy the soul as do murder and adultery. But the misfortune is that we govern ourselves in these not by what is sinful according to the principles of our faith, but by what is odious in the eyes of the world. We don't strive to avoid sin, but are content to avoid what is scandalous in it.

We are certainly under habits of pride until we are governed by humility, and we are not governed by humility until we deny ourselves and are afraid of every appearance of pride. No man is governed by religious justice until he is exact in all degrees of it and abhors every appearance of fraud and crafty management.

A common liar may hate some sort of lies, an unjust man may avoid some kinds of injustice, and a proud person may dislike some instances of pride. But these have no title to humility. It is not a single act or any particular restraint, but a uniform state of mind that stands constantly disposed to every degree of humility and is averse to every degree of pride that denominates one as being truly humble.

To measure any virtuous temper by any other standard than this is not to measure ourselves by true religion. How can anyone be said to be religiously chaste unless he abhors and avoids all instances of lewdness and impurity? Must it not, therefore, be the same in humility and every other virtue? Self-denial, then, is so universally essential that it is the foundation of every virtue, humility, and charity, calling for more self-contradiction than the strictest temperance.

Ambition and worldly cares distract the mind and fill it with false concerns. However, even these are in a nearer state to religion than idleness and indulgence. Ambition and worldly cares, though they employ the mind wrongly, preserve some degree of activity in it, which by some means may take a right turn. But idleness and indulgence are the death and burial of the soul.

I have been more severe upon this disposition because it is so common and is even acknowledged without shame. People who would not be thought of as reprobates are not afraid to let you know that they do little but eat and drink and sleep and take such diversions as suit with their ease. Yet such a state of life nourishes the corruption of our nature and exposes us to the vanity of the world.

"Watch and pray," said our Savior, "that ye fall not into temptation."[1] The devil's advice is to be idle and indulge; then you will yield to every temptation. If watching and prayer have any tendency to prevent our falling into temptation, it is certain that idleness and indulgence must in an equal degree make us incapable of resisting them.

How is it that Christianity cures the corruption of our nature? It does it by teaching us to live and act by principles of reason and righteousness. These are: first, God is our only good—we cannot possibly be happy but in enjoyment of Him as He reveals himself to us; second, our souls are immortal spirits that are here only in a state of trial and probation; third, we must all appear before the judgment seat of Christ to receive the sentence of eternal life or eternal death.

Judging and thinking, choosing and avoiding, hoping and fearing, loving and hating according to these principles becomes a creature sent to the world to prepare himself to live with God in everlasting happiness.

The happiness of true religion, which is a happiness in God alone, is a great contradiction to all our natural opinions, not only because it proposes a good which our senses cannot relish, but because it leads us from all those imaginary enjoyments to which our hearts have become attached.

We may let our senses tell us what we are to eat and drink or when we are to sleep; we may let them teach us how near we may draw

---

1. Matthew 26:41

to a fire or how great a burden we may carry or how deep we may go into the water. But if we appeal to them to know the true good for man, or what is our proper happiness, or what guilt there is in sin or what excellence there is in piety, we act as absurdly as if we were to try to hear with our eyes or see with our ears.

Religion, therefore, has as much power over us as it has power over our natural tempers, and the judgments of our senses so far as it has made us deny ourselves and reject the opinions of mere flesh and blood.

We judge everything in the same manner that the child judges his playthings; that is, with our senses alone, though we think that we act by reason. The world is made up of fine sights and pageantry which please and captivate the minds of men, because men have yet the minds of children. Often we laugh at the little pleasures and trifling satisfactions of children, but at the same time the wisdom and ambition and greatness of men are taken up with the same trifles.

Let us take another view of the weakness and disorder of our nature. When we see people drunk, or in a violent passion, we readily own that they are in a state of delusion—thinking, saying, and doing irregular things under the promptings of their high spirits. In these states we all see and acknowledge the power of our bodies over our reason and never suppose a man capable of judging or acting wisely as long as he is under the influence of violent passion or drink.

Whether a man be drunk with passion or strong drink, there is the same weakness of mind, the same disordered imagination, the same misapprehension of the nature of things.

We are always in a state either of self-love, pride, hatred, envy, covetousness or ambition. One or more of these passions affect in some degree our spirits in the same manner that liquor affects us. A silent envy, a secret vanity which nobody sees raises disorderly thoughts in our heads and perverts our judgments in the same manner as do more violent passions.

We see that a man who has enslaved himself to the pleasures of drinking and intemperance has rendered himself incapable of being a reasonable judge of other happiness and pleasure.

As the true way of knowing and being rightly affected by the weakness and mortality of our state is to view frequently the condition of dying men as pictures of ourselves, so the most likely means of affecting us with a just sense of the corruption and disorders of our hearts is to consider the frailties, corruptions, and disorders of others as certain representations of the frailty and corruption of our own state. When we see them, we may remember to review many plain reasons for resisting our own nature which has in it the seeds of all evil tempers.

If we see ourselves in the true light, we shall see the whole reason for Christian self-denial, for meekness and poverty of spirit, for putting off our old man, for renouncing ourselves that we may see all things in God. Religion has little or no hold upon us until we have these right apprehensions of ourselves. It may serve for a little decency of outward behavior, but it is not the religion of our hearts until we feel the weakness and disorders of our nature and embrace piety and devotion as the means of recovering us to a state of perfection and happiness in God.

XXVII.
The Invisible Union

Another tenet of our faith speaks of the "absolute necessity of divine grace." This, too, affords a universal and constant reason for self-denial. The invisible operation and assistance of God's Holy Spirit, by which we are disposed towards that which is good, and made able to perform it, is a confessed doctrine of Christianity.

Our natural life is preserved by some union with God, who is the fountain of life to all the creation. We do not know much about that union. We know that we are alive, for we are thinking beings, but how or by what influence from God our life is supported is a secret into which we cannot enter. It is the same thing with respect to our spiritual life. It arises from some invisible union with God which cannot be comprehended. Our Lord said, "The wind bloweth where it listeth and thou hearest the sound thereof, but cannot tell whence it cometh and whither it goeth; so is everyone that is born of God."[1] This shows us how ignorant we are of the manner of the operations of the Holy Spirit. We may feel His effects, as we may perceive the effects of the wind, but we are as much strangers to His manner of coming upon us as we are strangers to that exact point from whence the wind begins to blow and where it ceases.

The Spirit of God, like God the Father, is too high for our conceptions while we are in these dark houses of clay. But our Lord has in some degree helped our understanding of this by the manner of His giving the Holy Spirit to His disciples. "And He breathed on them and saith unto them, receive the Holy Ghost."[2] By this ceremony of breathing we are taught to conceive of the communications of the Holy Spirit with a likeness to breath, or wind, and that His influence comes upon us in a manner similar to a gentle breathing of air. Representations of the kind are only made in compliance with the weakness of our apprehensions, which not being able to conceive things as they are in their own nature, must be instructed by comparing them to such things as are familiar to our senses.

Thus, the wisdom and knowledge that are revealed from God are compared to light, not because light is a true representation of the wisdom of God, but because it serves best to represent it to our dull capacities. In like manner, the influences of the Holy Spirit are set forth by the ceremony of breathing upon us, not because breath, or air or wind, are true representations of the gifts of the Holy Spirit, but because they are the most proper representations that yet fall within our knowledge. But that which is most necessary for us to know, and of which we are sufficiently informed in Scripture, is the absolute necessity of divine assistance.

We are used to thinking of inspiration as applying to some extraordinary designs and acts of immediate revelation from God. As inspiration implies an immediate revelation from Him, in this sense there have been but few inspired persons. But inspiration that signifies an invisible operation or assistance and instruction of God's

---

1. John 3:8   2. John 20:22

Holy Spirit is the common gift and privilege of all Christians. In this sense of inspiration, they are all inspired. "Know ye not," said St. Paul. "that your body is the temple of the Holy Ghost which is in you."[3] Again, "Now if any man hath not the Spirit of Christ, he is none of his,"[4] and "For as many as are led by the Spirit of God, they are the sons of God."[5]

From these and many other similar passages, it is plain that the life we now live is a life in and by the Spirit of God, and that they are only sons of God who are led by this Spirit. This doctrine plainly proves the necessity of a constant self-denial, for it must be necessary that we deny ourselves all those tempers and ways of life which make God withhold His grace from us, and likewise all those enjoyments and indulgences which may make us less able and less disposed to improve and cooperate with that divine grace that is communicated to us.

Our blessed Lord said, "If any man love me, he will keep my words and my Father will love him, and we will come unto him and make our abode with him."[6] This teaches us how we are to invite the good Spirit of God to dwell in us. We are to prepare ourselves for the abode of this Divine Guest by loving Christ and keeping His commandments. We also learn that the Spirit of God does not equally visit all persons in all ways of life, but that we must prepare ourselves for His presence.

We are also told that "God resisteth the proud, and giveth grace to the humble."[7] This also explains to us the method of divine grace, that it is bestowed with regard to the state and temper of persons, that there are some dispositions which separate us from the Spirit of God and others that procure for us a larger share of His gifts and graces. We are also here taught to consider pride, not only as a sin having its particular guilt, but as one that extinguishes the divine light, deprives us of God's Spirit, and leaves us to sink under the corruption and weight of our nature.

We are to consider humility, also, not only as it is a reasonable duty and proper to our state, but as one that qualifies and prepares us for larger degrees of divine grace as may purify and perfect our souls

---

3. I Corinthians 6:19   4. Romans 8:9   5. Romans 8:14   6. John 14:23   7. I Peter 5:5

in all manner of holiness. All instances, therefore, of pride are to be avoided, all sorts of humily to be practiced, not only for their own sakes, but as necessary preparations for divine grace that we may be fit temples for the Holy Spirit to dwell in.

Seeing that we are none of Christ's if the Spirit of Christ be not in us, and that we are only Christians to the extent we are renewed by the Holy Spirit, nothing can be more necessary to true piety than that we form every part of our lives with regard to the Holy Spirit.

When we are left to consider our duty with relation to the express commandments of God, there are many ways of life which we think ourselves at liberty to follow because they seem to be no plain breach of any commandment. But we are to look to a further rule and to consider our pleasures and endeavors, not only as they are contrary to the letter of the law, but whether they are according to the Spirit of God. If they are contrary to Him, if they suit not with His secret inspirations, they are as truly to be avoided as if they were contrary to some express commandment. For we are assured from Scripture that they only are the sons of God who are led by the Spirit of God, and none can be said to be led by the Spirit of God but those whose lives conform to Him—whose actions, pleasures, hopes, and fears are such as may be said to be guided by the motions of the Holy Spirit.

We are, therefore, to consider ourselves as inspired persons who have no knowledge or wisdom but what comes from God and who know that this wisdom will dwell with us only as long as we act conformably with it. We vainly deceive ourselves by asking where is the harm of certain indulgences or vanities; we must consider whether they are such as are consistent with a life to be directed by the Holy Spirit, whether they will invite His assistance and make Him delight to dwell in us. In this manner must we examine all our ways of life, as well as our pleasures and inclinations.

People often think their designs and diversions innocent because they are not specifically sinful. But they should also consider whether they are vain and foolish and unsuitable to the state of a Christian. A life of folly and vanity and trifling designs is no more living by the Spirit of God than one of gross sins is keeping the commandments. The safest rule to judge of our actions is to consider them with relation to that Spirit by which we are to be guided. Is this design or act according to the wisdom and spirit of God? Am I in these things improving the secret inspiration of the Holy Spirit? Are these such as I can truly say I am led into them by the Spirit of God? Do I allow myself in them because they serve to set forth the glory of God and are agreeable to the condition of a disciple of Christ? This is the rule of perfection by which Christians are to regulate their thoughts and words and actions, for they are called by God to a state of purity and holiness to act by the motions of the Holy Spirit and make no other use of ourselves or the world we are in than what agrees with the dignity of life and state of glory to which we are called.

XXVIII.
The Marks of the New Life

The renewal of our hearts by the Spirit of God consists in new thoughts and new desires, in filling our minds with great and sublime truths, and in giving us desires and inclinations, hopes and fears, cares and pleasures suitable to them. This is being born of the Spirit. Hence there appears a plain reason for a universal self-denial, because the spirit of the world and the spirit of our corrupt hearts are in a state of contrariety to the Spirit and wisdom which are from above. It is the main business of our lives to contradict those motions of our hearts and tendencies of the world which are contrary to God's Spirit, which is the source of our new life in Christ.

If we would see anything exactly, we must take our eyes from everything else. If we would apprehend truly the things of religion, we must take our minds from all other objects. We see even in worldly matters that if we propose anything to a man when he is in pursuit of something else, he hardly hears or understands us; we must stay until such a time that his thoughts and passions are at rest.

This holds much more firmly in matters of religion. Its doctrines are neither heard nor understood because it always finds us in the pursuit of something else; the mind is employed wrongly when it centers upon any other happiness.

If we were to propose these truths to a man who is in a state of weariness, sickness, and approaching death, they would have quite another effect upon him. Then the great things of religion appear great indeed. He feels their whole weight and is amazed that he did not see them always in the same manner. It is the end of self-denial to put a stop to the follies of life and to mortify our passions that our souls may quietly consider and fully comprehend the truths which come from God, that our hearts being at liberty from a crowd of foolish thoughts may be ready to obey and cooperate with the inspirations of that Spirit which is to lead and quicken us in all holiness, that death and judgment, heaven and hell may make as deep impressions upon our minds in the middle of our lives as at our last hour, that we may be as wise and prudent as sick and dying men and live with such apprehensions as most people die with, that we may see the vanity of the world, the misery of sin, the greatness of eternity, and the want of God as those who stand upon the brink of another world.

This is the great and happy work of self-denial, which is to fill us with a spirit of wisdom to awaken us to a true knowledge of ourselves and show us who and where and what we are, until this self-denial has put a stop to our follies and opened our eyes to the realization that our life is but a sleep, a mere succession of shadows.

We are members of the Kingdom of God when the Kingdom of God is within us, when the spirit of religion is the spirit of our lives. When seated in our hearts, it diffuses itself into all our motions, principles, and thoughts. When we are wise by its wisdom, sober by its sobriety, and when we like and dislike, seek and avoid, mourn and rejoice as becomes those who are born of God, we act in accord with the work of the Holy Spirit. It is the work of the Holy Spirit to impart a new understanding, a new judgment, relish, and desire.

Therefore as we prepare ourselves by self-denial for this change of heart and mind, so far we invite the assistance and concur with the inspiration of the Holy Spirit. So far as we nourish any foolish passion, indulge any vanity of mind or corruption of heart, so far we resist the graces of God's Holy Spirit and render ourselves indisposed to relish and improve upon His secret inspirations. Christians are, therefore, to consider themselves not only as men who are to act by a principle of reason, but as spiritual beings who have a higher principle of life within them and who are to live by the wisdom and instructions of the Spirit of God.

As reasonable men would do everything that tended to strengthen and improve their reason, so wise Christians ought to practice every way of life that can fit them for further degrees of grace that can strengthen and preserve their union with the Spirit of God. For as a man without reason is but the figure of a man, so a Christian without the Spirit of God has but the form of a Christian. And as the perfection of a man consists in the highest improvement of his reason, so the perfection of a Christian consists in his growth in grace, in the spiritual turn and temper of his heart and mind. Here we must fix all our concern to remove all hindrances to divine grace and to preserve this Kingdom of God within us that we may be truly spiritual in all our ways and indulge in nothing that will lessen our union with the Spirit of God.

Seeing that this change of heart and newness of spirit is the whole of religion, we must fear all irregularity of spirit because it affects us in the seat of life and hurts us in our principal parts as to make us less capable of the graces and less obedient to the promptings of God's Holy Spirit. We ought to labor after a state of peace, satisfaction and thankfulness, and freedom from idle fears and false anxieties that our souls may be disposed to feel the joys, to rejoice in the comforts, to advance in the graces of the Holy Spirit.

With what care and exactness we are to conduct ourselves with regard to God's Spirit is set forth in the following words: "Let no corrupt communication proceed out of your own mouth but that which is good to the use of edifying, that it may minister grace unto the hearers, and grieve not the Holy Spirit of God, whereby ye are sealed unto the day of redemption."[1] That we may not here mistake what is meant by "corrupt communication", that we may not suppose it implies only sinful discourse, the Apostle adds, "But that which is

---

1. Ephesians 4:30

good to the use of edifying, that it may minister grace to the hearers."
It is a conversation that does not edify and profit the hearer that the
Apostle condemns as corrupt and to be avoided.

The Apostle does not prohibit this kind of conversation because
it is useless or impertinent, but for the reason that we may not grieve
the Holy Spirit. This shows us that we Christians are to govern
ourselves by no less a rule than a conformity to the Spirit of God, that
we are not only to deny ourselves vain and foolish actions, but also
idle and unedifying discourse, and conduct ourselves in all our
behavior with such a spirit of wisdom and purity as may make the
Holy Spirit *delight* to dwell in us. This rule of perfection is highly
conformable to the nature of our faith, for as our religion consists in a
new heart and a new spirit, it is certain that we are only then arrived to
the true state of our religion when it governs our words and actions at
all times and on all occasions.

Some people seem to know so little of religion that they confine
it to acts of devotion and public occasions of worship; they don't
consider that it consists of a new heart and new spirit, and that acts of
devotion, prayer and preaching, watchings, fastings, and sacraments
are only to fill us with this new heart and spirit and make it the
common constant spirit of our lives every day and in every place.

A man may be said to have some regard for religion who is
regular at places of divine worship, but he cannot be reckoned of a
religious spirit until it is his spirit in every place and on every
occasion—until he lives and breathes it, and thinks and speaks and
acts according to its motions.

If a person of pride and vanity in the general course of his life
should yet think himself humble because he had his appointed times
of praying for humility, we might say of him that he knew nothing of
the nature of that virtue. In like manner, if one whose conversation
and manner of life are not according to the spirit of religion, should
he yet think himself religious because he had his appointed places
of prayer, it might be justly said of him that he was a stranger to the
nature of true religion. For religion is not ours until we live by it,
until it is the religion of our thoughts, words, and actions, until it
goes with us into every place, sits uppermost on every occasion,
and forms and governs our hopes and fears, our cares and our

pleasures. He is the religious man who watches and guards his spirit and endeavors to be always in the attitude of religion that worships God in every place by a purity of behavior that is fearful of foolish thoughts and vain imaginations at one time as at another, and who is as wise and spiritual at home as in the house of God. When once true religion has possession of a man's heart, it is as agreeable to him at all times and in all places as it is to the ambitious man to act according to the dictates of ambition.

As we can do nothing without the Spirit of God, as He is our breath, our light, and our strength, so when we live in such a way as grieves and removes His Holy Spirit from us, we are as branches that are broken off from the tree and must perish in the deadness and corruption of our nature.

XXIX.
Holiness and Conversation

Let this therefore teach us to judge right of the sin and danger of vain, unedifying, and corrupt communication. It is not the sin of idleness or negligence, it is not the sin of a pardonable infirmity, it is not a little mistake in spiritual wisdom, but it is a sin that stands between us and the Tree of Life, that opposes our whole happiness, as it grieves and separates the Holy Spirit from us.

Let this also teach some people the reason why they are so dead and senseless of religion and hardly capable of an outward formal compliance with it. They are not guilty of gross sins, but at the same time they have no feeling or relish of religion. The reason is that they live in such an impertinence of conversation upon vain subjects that they render themselves unfit for the residence of the Holy Spirit. Their whole life is almost nothing but a course of that "filthiness, foolish talking, and jesting" which the Apostle forbids.[1]

1. Ephesians 5:4

This kind of conversation may grieve the Holy Spirit for two reasons. First, it proceeds from too disordered a soul for the Holy Spirit to delight in, for "out of the abundance of the heart the mouth speaketh."[2] Second, it is of a very great consequence and influence in life. We don't seem to apprehend enough either how much good or how much evil there is in conversation. I believe that the greatest instructions and the greatest corruptions proceed from it. If some people were to give us their true history, they would tell us that they never had any religion since they had certain acquaintances, and others have been led into a sincere piety only by conversing with pious people, for men's common conversation and ordinary life teach much more effectually than anything they say or do at set times and occasions.

When a clergyman preaches, he is for the most part considered as doing his duty according to his profession, whether it be good or bad. But if he is the same wise and virtuous man in his communication that he is in the pulpit, if his speech be seasoned with salt that it may minister grace to the hearers, if the common and ordinary actions of his life be visibly governed by a spirit of piety, he will make converts to holiness. He will be heard with reverence on Sundays not so much for the weight of what he says as for what he says and does all week. On the contrary, if a clergyman comes out of the pulpit and acts like other men, if he is irregular in his manner, trifling in his conversation, and as worldly in his pleasures as they, he will mightily lessen his power over the hearts of his hearers.

A father now and then gives his son virtuous advice, and the son perhaps is much the better for it, but when he never hears his father talking virtuously when he is giving advice, this makes him think that he is then only acting the part of a father, as when he is buying him clothes. On the other hand, if he sees his father's ordinary life and conversation to be under the rules of religion and his everyday conduct to be pious, it is very likely he will be won to an imitation of it.

One reason why a vain and unedifying conversation grieves the Holy Spirit may be not only that it proceeds from a corrupt heart, but

2. Matthew 12:34

that it does so much harm to those with whom we converse, for it is our communication, our manner of common life that affects others, either hardening them in sin or awakening them to a sense of piety. Let, therefore, all clergymen and heads of families look carefully to themselves; let them consider that if their daily life be vain and their conversation unedifying, they are not only in a corrupt state of heart themselves, but they are guilty of perverting the hearts of those over whom they wield special influence. Let them not think they have sufficiently discharged their duty by seeing that those who relate to them have their proper instructions, for it is next to impossible for such instructions to have their proper effect against the example of those we converse with.

If a clergyman plays and drinks with his flock on week days, let him not wonder if he preaches them asleep on Sundays. If a father swears and is intemperate and converses foolishly with his friends, let him not wonder that his children cannot be made virtuous. Almost all people will be such as those among whom they were born and bred.

We can neither live well nor ill to ourselves alone, but must of necessity do either good or harm to others by our manner of conversation. This is so infecting an evil that the Holy Spirit is readily grieved by it. This doctrine of abstaining from corrupt communication that we may not grieve the Spirit of God teaches a high aim and exalted degree of perfection which is peculiar to Christianity. As Christianity lays the design of uniting us to God and raising us to a more intimate participation of the divine nature, so we are to make this standard the rule of our perfection.

We must not only conduct ourselves by rules of morality, but pursue such degrees of purity as can only be expressed by an imitation of God and aspire after such wisdom as is suggested to us by our being temples of the Holy Spirit, and live like beings consecrated by the spirit of wisdom.

If we were to consider frequently the holy presence of this God within us and ask ourselves whether our discourse becomes one who is to act according to the inspirations of the Divine Spirit, we should find that the very thought of this dignity of our state would determine several points where no express law condemns us; we should find such a contrariety in many of our ways to our Christian greatness as would sufficiently check our behavior if only by showing that we acted beneath ourselves.

Some philosophers have exhorted man to reverence his reason as a ray of the Deity, but we can go much higher. We can exhort him to reverence the Deity that dwells in him and to act with such purity as becomes one who is inspired by the Holy Spirit, This is the improvement that we are to make of this doctrine of divine grace; it must make us exact and careful of our behavior that we may walk worthy of that Holy Spirit who dwells in us.[3]

XXX.
Devotion—A Habit of Mind

A principal tenet of our religion asserts that Christ is now at the right hand of God making perpetual intercession for us until the redemption of mankind is finished. Prayer, therefore, is a proper means of drawing near to God—a necessary method of restoring sinners to His favor, since He who has conquered sin and death, who is constituted Lord of all, is yet, as the great advocate for sinners, obliged to make perpetual intercession for them.

Whenever we are in the spirit of prayer, when our hearts are lifted up to God breathing out holy petitions to the throne of grace, we have the encouragement to be constant and fervent in it, that we are then joining with an intercession at the right hand of God and doing for ourselves on earth what our blessed Savior is doing for us in heaven. Who can consider his redemption as now carrying on by an

---

3. There follows in the original text two sections entitled "The Entertainment of the Stage" and "Reading Vain and Impertinent Books," which are here omitted. As one might expect, Law's objection to the theater and theater attendance was unequivocal, but in this he illustrates the contempt which many puritan-minded churchmen held for the licentious plays and playgoing during the Restoration and early eighteenth century . . . . The chapter on "Vain and Impertinent Books" is quite general and more of a long digression than an integral part of the work.

intercession in heaven without feeling himself agreeable to God when the constancy of his prayers bears some resemblance to the Lord's constant activity? This shows us also that we are most of all to desire those prayers which are offered up at the altar where the body and blood of Christ are joined with them, for as our prayers are only acceptable to God through the merits of Jesus Christ, so we may be sure that we are praying to God in the most prevailing way when we pray in the name of Christ and plead His merits in the highest manner we can.

Devotion may be considered either as an exercise of public or private prayers at set times and occasions, or as a state of mind, and disposition of the heart which is rightly affected with such exercises.

External acts of devotion are very liable to falseness and are only so far good as they proceed from a right disposition of heart and mind. As zealous professions of friendship are but the more abominable hypocrisy for being often repeated unless there be an equal zeal of heart, so solemn prayers, likewise, are but repeated hypocrisies unless the heart and mind be conformable to them. Since it is the heart only that is devout, I shall consider devotion chiefly as a state and attitude of the heart, for it is in this sense only that Christians are called to a constant state of devotion. They are not to be always on their knees in acts of prayer, but they are to be always in the state and spirit of devotion.

Friendship does not require us to be always waiting upon our friends in external services; these have their times and seasons of intermission. It is only the service of the heart, the friendship of the mind that is never to intermit. It is not to begin and end as external services do, but is to persevere in a constancy like the motion of the heart, or the beating of the pulse. It is just so in devotion. Prayers have their hours, their beginning and ending, but the disposition of the heart towards God, which is the life and spirit of prayer, is to be as constant and lasting as our own life and spirit.

The repeating of a creed at certain times is an act of faith, but the faith which overcomes the world stays neither for times nor seasons, but is a living principle of the soul that is always believing, trusting, and depending upon God. In the same manner, verbal prayers are acts of devotion. But that prayer which saves and opens the gates of heaven stops not at forms and manuals of devotion, but is a language of the soul—a judgment of the heart which worships, adores, and delights in God at all times and seasons.

The need for prayer is, like all other duties of piety, founded in the nature of God, as He is the sole fountain of all happiness; it is founded in the nature of man, as he is weak and helpless and full of wants. Prayer is an earnest application or ascent of the heart to God as to the sole cause of all happiness.

He, therefore, who most truly feels the misery, corruption, and weakness of his own nature, is most fully convinced that a relief from these disorders and true happiness are to be found in God alone. He who is most fully convinced of these truths is most fully possessed of the spirit of prayer.

There is but one way to arrive at a true state of devotion, and that is to get right notions of ourselves and of the divine nature, that having a full view of the relation we bear to God, our souls may as constantly aspire after Him as they constantly aspire after happiness. This also shows us the absolute necessity of all those forementioned doctrines of humility and renunciation of the world, for if devotion is founded in a sense of the poverty, misery, and weakness of our nature, then nothing can more effectually destroy the spirit of devotion than pride, vanity, and indulgence of any kind. These stop the breath of prayer and extinguish the flame of devotion as water extinguishes common fire.

If prayer is also founded in right notions of God, in believing Him to be the sole cause of all our happiness, then everything that takes this truth out of our minds, or makes us less sensible to it, makes us far less capable of devotion. Hence worldly cares, false satisfactions, and vain pleasures are to be renounced that we may be able to pray; the spirit of prayer has no further hold of us than so far as we see our wants and imperfections, and likewise the infinite fullness and all-sufficiency of God. When we thoroughly feel these two great truths, then are we in the true spirit of prayer.

Would you, therefore, be in the state of devotion, you must practice all those ways of life that may humble you in your own sight; you must forbear all those indulgences and vanities which blind your heart and give you false notions of yourself; you must seek that way of life and accustom yourself to such practices as may best convince you of the vanity of the world and the littleness of everything but God. This is the only foundation of prayer. You can desire it only in such a degree as you feel you want it. It is certain, therefore, that whatever lessens or abates the feeling of your wants, whatever takes you from looking to God as the only possible relief of them so far lessens the spirit and fervor of your devotion.

We sometimes exhort people to fervor in devotion, but this can only mean the outward acts of it, for to exhort people to be fervent in devotion as implies a temper of heart is to as little a purpose as to exhort them to be merry or sorry. The only way to be devout is to view God and our own condition in the way our Lord and His disciples viewed them.

It is impossible for a man to grieve when he finds his condition answering his desires; neither can he be overjoyed when he finds his state to be full of misery. Yet this is as possible and consistent with our nature as for a man to aspire after and delight in God as his only happiness while he is delighting in himself and the vanity of the world. To pretend to great devotion without great humility and an entire renunciation of all worldly tempers is to pretend to impossibilities. It is as if a man should pretend to be cheerful while he is in vexation and impatience. He must first bring himself to a state of satisfaction and contentment, and then cheerfulness will flow from it. So he who would be devout must first be humble, have a full view of his own miseries and wants and the vanity of the world, and then his soul will be full of desires after God.

Again, suppose you were to call a man from a joyful feast, from pleasures of songs, music and dancing, and tell him to go into the next room to grieve for half an hour and then to return to his mirth. You may tell him that to mourn is a very excellent thing and highly becoming to a rational creature. It is possible he might obey you as far as to go into the room appointed for mourning; he may sit still, look grave, sigh and hang his head and stay out his half hour. But you are sure he cannot really grieve for this reason: he is in a state of festival joy and hopes to return to the feast.

This is the state of great numbers of Christians. They are always at a feast; their lives are nothing but a succession of such pleasures and satisfactions as affect and hurry their minds like the festival joys of drinking, music, and dancing. When they go to devotions, they are just as capable of it as the man who is rejoicing at the feast is capable of mourning at the same time. Let not the reader think this is the case only of people of great means; it applies equally to those in lower stations of life.

Whoever, therefore, finds himself unable to relish strains of devotion may be certain that it is owing to the way of life he is in. He may also be assured that his life is wanting in the virtues of humility, self-denial, and renunciation of worldly goods since these virtues as naturally prepare and dispose the soul to aspire after God as a sense of sickness disposes one to wish for health.

It has been shown that devotion as an attitude of mind must have something to produce it. We know it is not all-important how many religious books we have read or even how often we have gone to church and felt a measure of fervor in our prayers; these are uncertain signs. But we must look to the foundation and assure ourselves that our hearts harbor no love of the world. If our humility is false or our worldly tempers half mortified, our devotion will be in the same state of falseness and imperfection. We must alter our lives in order to alter our hearts, for it is impossible to live one way and pray another.

This may teach us to account for the several false kinds of devotion which appear in the world. They cannot be other than what they are, because they have no foundation to support them. Devotion is like friendship; you hear of it everywhere, but find it nowhere. In like manner, devotion is everywhere to be seen in modes of worship, in forms of speech, but is in reality scarcely to be found. Also, you see as much difference in the devotion itself as in the faces of Christians, for without the true foundation, it appears like affected friendship— in many shapes.

Devotion, we see, is an earnest application of the soul to God as its only happiness. All those texts of Scripture which call us to God as our true and only good, and exhort us to fullness of faith, of hope, of joy, and trust in God are to be considered as exhortations to devotion, because devotion is only another name for the exercise of these virtues.

XXXI.
Incentives to Devotion

That soul is devoted to God which constantly rises towards God in habits of love, faith, hope, joy, and trust. The end and design of religion, as it proposes to raise a man to a life of glory with Christ at the right hand of God, carries a stronger reason for devotion than any particular exhortation to prayer. "Beloved," said St. John, "It doth not yet appear what we shall be, but we know that when He shall appear, we shall be like Him, for we shall see Him as He is."[1] St. Paul also said, "As we have born the image of the earthy, we shall also bear the image of the heavenly."[2]

Such texts as these seem to me to carry the most powerful motives to awaken the soul to a state of devotion, for as the Apostle says, "Every man that hath this hope purifieth himself, even as He is pure."[3] So he who has this hope of being taken into so glorious an enjoyment of the divine nature must find his heart raised and enlivened by thinking upon God. These truths cannot be believed without putting the soul into a state of prayer, adoration, and joy in God.

It was this view of future glory that made the Apostle Peter break out in this strain of thanksgiving, "Blessed be the God and Father of our Lord Jesus Christ, which . . . hath begotten us to a lively hope by the resurrection of Jesus Christ from the dead, To an inheritance undefiled and that fadeth not away. . . ."[4] If we would praise and adore God with such thanksgiving as filled the heart of the Apostle Peter, we must raise it by a contemplation of the same truth: the incorruptible inheritance that is prepared for us.

---

1. I John 3:2   2. I Corinthians 15:49   3. I John 3:3   4. I Peter 1:3,4

Again, the apostle Paul said to the Philippians, "Our conversation is in heaven," and as reason and motive to this heavenly conversation he adds, "Whence we look for the Savior, the Lord Jesus Christ, who shall change our vile body that it may be fashioned like unto his glorious body."[5] Hence, the most powerful motive to heavenly-mindedness, the plainest reason for our conversation in heaven, is our expectation of Christ's glorious appearance, when He shall come to put an end to the miseries of this life and clothe us with robes of immortality. These truths much more effectually raise the heart to God than any particular precepts to prayer; they do not so much exhort as carry the soul to devotion: he who feels these truths feels himself devout; they leave a light upon the soul which will kindle into holy flames of love and delight in God.

The way, therefore, to live in true devotion is to live in the contemplation of these truths. We must daily consider the end and hope of our calling that our minds may be formed and raised to such desires as are suitable to it, that all little anxieties, worldly passions, and vain desires may be swallowed up in one great desire for future glory. When our heart is in this state, then it is in a state of devotion, tending to God in such a manner as justly suits the nature of our religion. For where should our hearts aspire but where our treasure is?

This devotion to God is signified in Scripture as living by faith and not by sight—when the invisible things of the other life are the reason, motive, and measure of our constant desires. When Christians are thus settled in right judgments of things and tend towards God in such motions and desires as are suitable to them, then are they devout worshippers of God everywhere; this makes the common actions of their lives acts of religion and turns every place into a chapel. And it is to this state of devotion that we are called, not only by particular precepts, but by the whole nature and tenor of our religion.

As states of the mind and heart must be supported by actions and exercises suitable to them, so devotion, which is an earnest application of the soul to God as its only happiness, must be

---

5. Philippians 3:20-21

supported and kept alive by actions and exercises suitable to it—that is, by hours and forms of prayer both public and private. The devotion of the heart disposes us to observe set times of prayer, and on the other hand to set times of prayer as naturally increase and enliven the devotion of the heart. It is like this in other cases: habits of the mind dispose us to actions suitable to them, and these actions likewise strengthen and improve the habits from which they proceed.

It is the habitual taste for music that takes people to concerts, and again it is concerts that increase the habitual love of music. It is the right disposition of the heart towards God that leads people to outward acts of prayer which preserve and strengthen the right disposition of the heart towards God. As we are to judge the significance of our prayers by looking to the state of our heart, so are we to judge of the state of our heart by looking to frequency, constancy, and importunity of our prayers. For as we are sure that our prayers are insignificant unless they proceed from a right heart, so unless our prayers are frequent, constant, and full of importunity may we be equally sure that our heart is not right towards God.

XXXII.
Importunity to Prayer

Our Lord has indeed condemned one sort of long prayer: "But when ye pray, use not vain repetitions as the heathen do, for they think they shall be heard for their much speaking."[1] It is not length or a continuance of prayer that is here forbidden, but vain repetitions when the same words are only repeated. Also, the heathen are not here condemned for being importunate and persevering in their prayer, but for a wrong judgment, a false devotion in that they thought they were heard because they spoke much

---

1. Matthew 6:7

by merely repeating the same words. All that Christians are here forbidden is thinking that the efficacy of prayer consists in vain and long repetitions; they are to employ a better principle. Some people conclude wrongly from this that shortness is a necessary qualification of prayer.

How willing must such people be to be deceived in such a matter. The length or shortness of prayer is not the point at all. To think that a short prayer is better because it is short is the same error as the heathen's which contends that a prayer is more powerful the longer the same words are repeated; it is the same mistake in the nature of devotion.

Suppose the meaning of these words was something obscure; surely the Lord has expressly taught and recommended a continuance and importunity in prayer elsewhere. Can He who so often retired to deserts and mountains and solitary places to pray, who spent whole nights in prayer, be supposed to have left a reproof upon those who would follow His example? Besides the authority of His great example, His teaching is also plain:

> He spake a parable unto them to this end, that men ought always to pray and not to faint. There was in a city a judge which feared not God nor regarded man. And there was a widow in that city, and she came unto him saying, "Avenge me of my adversary." And He would not for awhile. But afterwards he said to himself, "Though I fear not God, nor regard man, yet because this widow troubleth me, I will avenge her . . . and shall not God avenge his own elect which cry day and night unto Him?[2]

We are told that this parable was to teach men to pray always and not to faint. It is plain that it has no other intent but to recommend continuance and importunity as the most prevailing qualifications of prayer. The widow is relieved, not because she asked relief, but because she continued to ask for it, and God is said to avenge His elect not because they cry to Him now and then, but because they cry day and night.

Our blessed Lord teaches the same doctrine in another parable.

2. Luke 18:1-7

A person goes to his friend to borrow three loaves of him at midnight. It concludes, "I say unto you, though he would not rise and give him because he is his friend, yet because of his importunity he will rise and give him as many as he needeth."[3] Here again, the sole scope of this passage is to show the great power and efficacy of continuance and importunity in prayer.

St. Paul commands further not only to pray but to "pray without ceasing."[4] Also, "praying always with all prayer and supplication in the Spirit."[5] and "continue in prayer."[6]

Our Savior said, "But thou, when thou prayest, enter into thy closet, and when thou hast shut thy door, pray unto thy Father . . . ."[7] Here is no mention of the time of prayer, but this preparation, this entering into our closet and shutting the door seems to teach us that it is a work of some time, that we are not hastily to open our door, but are to allow ourselves time to continue and be importunate in our prayers.

How long and how often all people ought to pray is not to be stated by one particular measure. But we may take as a general rule that every Christian is to pray often and as long to show a perseverance and importunity in prayer that indicates he prays "without ceasing." One would think it impossible for people to be sparing in their devotions if they have read the parables of our Lord which teach us that the blessings of heaven and the gifts and graces of the Holy Spirit are given to those who persist in prayer.

Here is a brief argument in favor of frequent and continued prayers.

First, frequent and continued prayers are a likely means to beget in us the spirit of prayer. A man who is often in his closet on his knees before God, though he may for some time perform but a "lip-labor," will, if he perseveres, find the very labor of his lips altering the temper of his heart and that he has learned to pray by praying often.

This we find to be true in all parts of life. We catch a spirit and manner from such conversation and actions as we allow ourselves in. Use is called a second nature, and experience teaches us that whatever

---

3. Luke 11:8 4. I Thessalonians 5:17 5. Ephesians 6:18 6. Colossians 4:2 7. Matthew 6:6

we accustom ourselves to will by degrees transform our spirit into a likeness to it.

Everything that we practice habitually enters into our nature in this manner and becomes a part of us before we are aware. Notice how some people tell a story so long that they forget they have invented it. This is not because they have a bad memory, but rather that the things which are constant and familiar will by degrees steal the approbation of the heart. If, therefore, we would but be often on our knees, putting up our prayers to God, though for awhile it was only form and outward compliance, yet our hearts would by degrees learn the language from our mouths. The subjects of our prayers would become the subject of our hearts; we should pray ourselves into devotion, and it would become a part of us in the same manner that all other ways enter into our nature. Our reason and judgment would at last consent to our lips, and by saying the same things often we should come to believe and feel them in the proper manner.

Another great advantage in frequent and constant prayers is that the cares and pleasures of life and the levity, vanity, and dullness of our minds make us to some extent unfit for devotion. We enter into our closets unprepared for prayer. If our petitions are very short, we shall end our prayers before our devotion is begun—before we have time to collect our minds or turn our hearts to the business we are upon.

Continuance in prayer is a great deterrent to these indispositions, not only as it gives the heart leisure to fall from worldly cares and concerns, but as it exercises the mind upon those subjects as are likely to abate its vanity and distraction and raise it into a state of seriousness and attention. All people tend to inconstancy in prayer; they join heartily in some petitions and wander away from others. It is therefore but common prudence to continue our prayers that our minds, which tend to wander, may return to spiritual matters.

If we were masters of our attention sufficiently to be as fervent as we pleased, fewer words would be adequate for our devotion. But since our minds are weak, inconstant, and to some extent ungovernable, we must endeavor to catch and win them to devotion by such means as are suited to a state of weakness, dullness, and inconstancy. He who goes to his closet in a hurry, only to repeat a short form of words, may pray all his life without any devotion. If a man were to make it a law to himself to meditate awhile before he begins his prayers if he were to force his mind to think what prayer is, what he prays for and to whom he prays if he should again make it a rule to stop in some part of his prayer to ask his heart whether it really prays, or to let his soul rise in silence towards God, he would assist by such meditation in rendering the heart truly devout.

It is not intended by this to impose any particular method upon all people; it is only to show us that there are certain means, though small in themselves, that are most helpful in making our minds attentive and fervent towards God.

It is the business of every sincere Christian, therefore, to be as wise as he can in these self-disciplines. As we know the falseness of our own hearts and the occasions of our defects, it is wise for us to think upon the amendments of our hearts as demanding the most helpful rules possible. Self-reflection is the shortest and most certain way of becoming truly wise and truly pious.

XXXIII.
Aids to Prayers

There are at least two seasons of the heart which, if we would but reflect upon, might give us such knowledge of ourselves as to assist our devotions and the time we are most indisposed to pray. First, reflect how it was with you, what circumstances you were in, what you had been doing, what you were thinking about when you were deeply affected in your devotions previously. If you remember the state you were in when you were disposed to pray fervently, you may be assisted in raising your devotion at another time. As you recall the same thoughts and do what you did before, you may again produce the same effects. It would help to put down in writing short remembrances of the chief things that raised your heart to fervency in prayer.

On the contrary, when you find yourself much indisposed to prayer, reflect upon what state you were in and what happened to you and what thoughts were in your head and what passions were then awakened. When you recall the state you were in when your devotions were hindered previously, you may decide what to avoid in order to keep yourself in an attitude of devotion. Again, if you were to make notes in writing of the chief things that caused indisposition to prayer, you would have a constant and faithful source of information of what ways of life you must avoid.

Frequent and continued prayer is the best remedy against the power of sin. I do not mean it procures the divine grace and assistance except as it convinces, instructs, and fortifies the mind against all sin. Every endeavor to pray is an endeavor to feel the truth of our prayers, to convince our minds of the reasonableness and fitness of those things that are the subject of our prayers so that he who prays most is one who labors most to convince his heart and mind of the guilt, deformity, and misery of sin. Prayer, therefore, considered merely as an exercise of the heart upon such subjects, is the most certain way to destroy the power of sin, for so far as we pray, so far we renew our convictions, enlighten our minds, and fortify our hearts by fresh resolutions.

If prayer at all convinces the mind, frequency and continuance in prayer must be the most certain way to establish the mind in a steady, well-grounded state of conviction. They who are for short prayers because they suppose God does not need much entreaty, ought also to show that the heart of man does not need assistance of much prayer, that it is so regular and uniform in its tendency to God, so full of right judgments and good motions as not to need that strength and light which arises from much praying. Unless this be the state of our hearts, we shall want much prayer to move and awaken us.

If, therefore, men would consider prayer, not only as an invocation to God, but also as an exercise of holy thoughts, and an endeavor to feel and be affected by the great truths of religion, they would soon see that though God is so good as not to need much calling upon, yet man is so weak as to be under constant need of that help and light and improvement which arise from praying much.

It is perhaps for this reason that God promises to give to those who are importunate. If God does not give to us at our first asking, it is not because our prayers make any change in God, but rather that our importunity has made a change in us. It has altered our hearts and rendered us proper objects of God's gifts and graces.

When we would know how much we ought to pray, we must consider how much our hearts need to be altered and remember that the great work of prayer is to work upon ourselves. It is not only to move and affect God, but it is to move and affect our own hearts and fill them with such tempers as God delights to reward.

Prayer is never so good a preservation against sin or a corrective of the heart as when we extend it to all the particularities of our life. Enumerating all our wants, infirmities, and disorders is not to inform God, but it is a means of informing ourselves; it acquaints our hearts in the best manner with our true condition. When our prayers descend to the circumstances of our whole condition, they become a faithful mirror to us by which we see ourselves in a true light.

Don't be content, therefore, with confessing yourself to be a sinner, or with praying against sin in general; but when you see yourself as you really are, if you pray constantly against such particular sins as you find yourself most subject to, the frequent sight of your own sins and your constant deploring of their guilt will give your prayers ready entrance into your heart and put before you means of mending your life.

If you confess yourself only to be a sinner, you only confess yourself to be a man, but when you describe and confess your own particular guilt, then you find cause for your own particular sorrow; then you give your prayers all the power they can have to affect and wound your heart. In like manner, when you pray for God's grace, don't be satisfied with a general petition, but make your prayers suitable to your defects and continue to ask for such gifts and graces of the Holy Spirit as you find yourself defective in. This will not only give life to your petitions and make your heart go along with them, but will also be the surest means to fit and prepare you for such graces as you pray for.

Particularity in our prayers is also the greatest trial of the *truth* of our hearts. A man may think he prays for humility because he has the word *humility* in his prayers. But if he were to branch humility into all its separate manifestations, he would not likely be disposed to pray for them. For instance, if he were to represent to himself the several particulars which make a man poor in spirt, he would not find his heart desirous of them. The only way to know the truth of our hearts and whether we really pray for any virtue is to make our petitions for specific illustrations of virtue. If the proud man were to pray daily for humility and to beg God to remove him from all occasions of such pride that were contrary to humility, he would find that such prayers would either conquer the pride or his pride would put an end to his prayers.

Everyone may make his private devotions useful to him if he has but piety enough to intend it, for everyone may know his own state if he will. We commonly say that people are blind to themselves. We pass this judgment because we see them pretending to many virtues and declaiming against vices to which they are the most subject.

We see people often pretending to be rich. This is not because they don't know their state, but because they would not have you to know it. This is the case in all other pretenses. The false, the proud, the worldly man who pretends to fidelity, humility, and heavenly affection knows that he is none of these.

He who has learned to pray has learned the greatest secret of a holy and happy life. If we direct our hearts into any other way, they will return to us again empty and weary. Time will convince the vainest and blindest minds that happiness is no more to be found in the things of this world than it is to be dug out of the earth. But when the motions of our hearts are motions of piety, tending to God in constant acts of devotion, love, and desire, then we have found rest unto our souls; then it is that we have conquered the misery of our nature and neither love nor desire in vain; then it is that we have found out a Good that is suited to our natures and equal to all our wants—one that will fill us with peace and joyful expectations here and eternal happiness hereafter. For he who lives in the spirit of devotion, whose heart is always full of God, lives at the top of human happiness and is the furthest removed from all the vanities and vexations which disturb the weary minds of men who are devoted to the world.

XXXIV.
Imitation of Christ

Our religion teaches us that as we have "borne the image of the earthly, so we shall bear the image of the heavenly"[1]—that after our death we shall rise to a state of life and happiness like to that which our blessed Savior enjoys at the right hand of God. Since it is the great end of our religion to make us fellow-heirs with Christ and partakers of the same happiness, it is no wonder that our faith should require us to be like Christ in this life and to imitate His example.

How can we think we are going to be with our Lord and be as He is forever unless we conform to His Spirit in this life and endeavor to be what He was when He was here? Let us observe that the nature of our religion teaches us this duty in a more convincing manner than any precepts one might follow. We need not look for particular texts of Scripture which command us to imitate the life of Christ, for the very end and design of our religion is to make us one with Christ through partaking of His life. Hence, we are called to be one with Him here and to be partakers of the same spirit and manner exemplified by Him on earth.

When it is said that we are to imitate the life of Christ, it does not mean that we are called to the same kind of life exactly as He lived it, for this cannot be. But it is certain we are called to the same spirituality that characterized our Savior's life and actions. We are to be like Him in heart and mind, to act by the same rule, to look towards the same end, and to govern our lives by the same spirit. This

---

1. Corinthians 15:49

is an imitation of Jesus Christ which is as necessary to salvation as it is to believe on His name. This is the sole end of all the counsels, commands, and doctrines of Christ.

As no doctrines are true but such as are according to the doctrines of Christ, so it is equally certain that no life is Christian but that which is according to the pattern and example of the life of Christ. He lived as infallibly as He taught, and it is as irregular to vary from His example as it is false to dissent from His doctrines. To live as He lived is certainly the one sole way of living as we ought as to believe what He taught is the one sole way of believing as we ought.

Jesus said, "I am the way, the truth, and the life; no man cometh unto the Father but by me."[2] Christians often hear these words and think they have fulfilled them by believing in Jesus Christ. But they should consider that when Jesus said He is the way, He meant that His way of life is the way all Christians are to live, that it is by living after the manner of His life that any man comes to the Father. The doctrine of this passage teaches that however we may call ourselves Christians or disciples of Christ, we cannot come to God the Father but by entering into that way of life which was the way of our Savior's life.

Some may say that Jesus was the Savior of the world, that He was born to redeem mankind in a condition so different from ours that being the Son of God, He lived far above what may be considered a rule for our live. To this it may be answered that although Christians are not redeemers of the world as He was, although they do not have His extraordinary powers, yet they have their work to do in the manner that He did His. They have their part which must be performed with obedience to God and regard for His glory— with such good holy dispositions as our Lord manifested in every part of His life.

2. John 14:6

XXXV.
Members of One Body

The poor widow's mites were but a small matter in themselves, but as they were the utmost she could give, our Savior set them above the larger contribution of the rich. This may encourage people in every state of life to be contented with their capacity for doing good, provided they but act up to it. Let no one think that he is too low or mean to follow his Lord in the salvation of souls. Let him but add his mite, and if it is all that he has, he will be thought to have done much.

All are not to be preachers or teachers of religion any more than all are to be apostles or prophets or workers of miracles. Christians are like members of the same body; they are different from each other as hands and eyes have different offices to perform, yet their different parts serve and prompt the common end. As the "eye cannot say to the hand, I have no need of thee: nor again the head to the feet, I have no need of you,"[1] so neither can the learned teacher say he has no need of the unlearned person. The work of salvation is carried on by all hands, as well by him who is taught as by him who teaches. An unlearned person, by being desirous of instruction and careful to comply with it, may by this disposition promote salvation to as great extent as he who is able and willing to instruct.

This teachable disposition may more effectively draw others to a like manner than another man's ability and care for teaching. In many instances the success of a teacher is owing more to the manner and example of the one being taught than to the strength of the teacher.

---

1. I Corinthians 12:21

Hence, as the Apostle says, all do not have the gifts of healing and all do not speak in tongues, yet all have some part that they may perform in the salvation of mankind. It is not only the business of clergymen, but all are engaged in the same business, though not in the same manner. Had the poor widow excused herself from taking care of the treasury by thinking only the rich were to contribute towards it, she would have missed the great commendation bestowed upon her by our Lord. While some widows may be so poor that they do not have so much as a mite and must content themselves, therefore, with the charity of their hearts, this can never happen in the business of salvation where none can be so poor or destitute as not to have a mite to contribute towards it. No circumstances of life can hinder us from being examples of piety and goodness to all who are about us.

This is the great way in which we are to follow the example and spirit of our Savior. He came to save the world and to raise mankind to a happiness in heaven; we, also, must consider ourselves as called to carry on this great work and to concur in this glorious design.

The Apostle said, "Destroy not him with thy meat for whom Christ died."[2] We may reason justly with ourselves that as it lies much in our power to hinder salvation, so it must be in our power to an equal degree to edify and promote the salvation of those whom Jesus Christ died to save. Destroy not, therefore, by your negligence, impatience, or want of care that relation for whom Christ died, nor think you have done enough to save those who relate to you until there is no more you can do for them. This is the state in which all Christians are to consider themselves as appointed by God in their several stations to carry on the great work for which Christ came into the world.

Ministers are not the only men who have a cure for souls, but every Christian has some people around him whose salvation he is obliged to be careful of, with whom he is to live in all godliness and purity. All Christians, no matter what their station in life, must consider themselves as hired by Christ to work in His vineyard, for no circumstances of life can hinder them from promoting the salvation of others.

2. Romans 14:15

It may be that God has not appointed you as prophet; yet you need not fall short of happiness, for our Savior has said, "He that receiveth a prophet in the name of a prophet shall receive a prophet's reward."[3] This shows us that though all men have not the same part to act in the common salvation, yet none will be losers by that state they are in if they but be true to the particular duties of it. If they do all the good they can in their particular state, they will be looked upon with such acceptance as the poor widow who gave all that she had.

XXXVI.
Perfection in Spirit

THERE IS no falseness of our hearts that leads us into greater errors than imagining that we shall some time or other be better than we are now. Perfection has no dependence upon external circumstances; it wants no times or opportunities, but it is in its highest state when we are making the best use of that condition in which we are now placed.

The poor widow did not stay until she was rich before she contributed to the treasury. She readily brought her mite, little as it was, and it got her the reward and commendation of great charity. We must imitate the wisdom of the poor widow and exercise every virtue in the same manner that she exercised her charity. We must stay for no time or opportunities, wait for no change of life or fancied abilities, but remember that every time is a time for piety and perfection.

Let us not vainly say that if we had lived in the days of our Lord, we would have followed Him, or that if we could work miracles, we would devote ourselves to His glory. To follow Christ as far as we can in our present state and to do all we are able for His glory is as

---

3. Matthew 10:41

acceptable to Him as if we were working miracles in His name.

The greatness we are to aim at is not the greatness of our Lord's actions, but it is in the greatness of His spirit and manner in all areas of our lives. Every state of life, whether public or private, may be conducted and governed by the same spirit that Christ displayed; hence every state of life may be Christ-like. "Learn of me," said our blessed Lord, "for I am meek and lowly in heart."[1] He does not say, "Be ye in the state and condition I am in," for that is impossible. Yet He calls on us to be like Him in meekness and lowliness of heart and spirit and to emulate the same spirit that characterized His entire life. So far as we can discover the wisdom, purity, and heavenliness of His designs, so far we have learned what His ways are like.

In all our actions and ways of life we must appeal to this rule. We must reckon ourselves no further as living like Christians than we live like Christ. We may be assured that so far as we depart from the Spirit of Christ, so far we depart from the state to which He has called us, for the blessed Jesus has called us to live as He did and to walk in the same spirit that He walked that we may be in the same happiness with Him when this life is at an end.

When our Lord was upon the cross, He prayed for his enemies as follows: "Father, forgive them, for they know not what they do."[2] Now all Christians readily acknowledge that this attitude of Christ is to be the standard of our attitude on a similar occasion. We ought not to fall short of it, but must be perfectly like Christ in this charity towards our murderers. For the very same reason, every other spirit of Christ is as much the exact rule of all Christians as His attitude towards His murderers.

Is it not as good an argument to say we are to be disposed towards the world and worldly enjoyments as Christ was? He was as right in one case as the other, and no more erred in His temper towards worldly things than in His attitude towards His enemies. Would we not fail to be good Christians if we fell short of that forgiving spirit which the blessed Savior showed upon the cross? And shall we not equally fail to be good Christians if we fall short of

1. Matthew 11:29   2. Luke 23:34

that humble and meek spirit which He showed in all His life? Can anyone say why the spirit of Christ towards His enemies should be more than the exact measure of our spirit upon similar occasions?

If the reader can find a reason why he may forgive his enemies less than Christ forgave His or be wanting in humility, meekness, charity towards his enemies, and other qualities of perfection, then he may own he may be a Christian without the spirit that characterized Christ. But he will find that not living in that meekness and lowliness of heart, in that disregard of the world, that love of God, that self-denial and devotion in which our Savior lived, is to be as unlike Him as he who dies completely without Christian knowledge.

The spirit and manner of Christ is the strict measure of the spirit and manner of all Christians. It is not in a particular aspect of His life that we are to follow His example, but we are to aspire after His whole spirit, to be in all things as He was, and to think it as dangerous to depart from His spirit and manner in one instance as in another.

The same authority in all our Savior did obliges us to conform to His whole example: why should we have more value for this world than He had? What is there in our circumstances that make it more proper for us to have more affection for the things of this life than He? Is the world any more our happiness than it was His? Are riches, honors, and pleasures any more our proper good than they were His? Are we any more born for this life than He was? Are we in less danger of being corrupted by its enjoyments than He was? Are we more at leisure to take up our time in worldly satisfactions than He was? Have we a work upon our hands that we can more easily finish than He could finish His? As this world is as little our happiness and more our danger than it was His, as we have a work to finish that requires all our strength that is as contrary to the world as was His, it is plain that there was no necessity for His disregard of the world that does not apply to us in a similar way.

Our Lord said, "I came down from heaven, not to do my own will, but the will of Him that sent me."[3] Can any Christian show why he may think otherwise of himself than our Savior thought here? Or

---

3. John 6:38

that he need be less devoted to the glory of God than He was? What is there in our nature and condition to make any difference? Do we not stand in the same relation to God that our Savior did? Have we not the same nature that He had? Can anything else be the happiness of our nature than was the happiness of His? Was He a loser of true happiness by devoting Himself to the will of God? Or can this be our case, though it was not His? Was it not the greatness and happiness of our Lord that He lived in God alone? And is there any other happiness or greatness for us but by making the end and aim of our life the same as was His?

XXXVII.
Perfection in Christ-likeness

CHRIST DID NOT mistake the nature of man or of the world; He did not overlook any real felicity or pass by any solid good. He only made the best use of human life and made it the cause of all the happiness and glory that can arise from it. To find a reason why we should live otherwise than He lived, why we should seek less the glory of God than He sought it, is to find a reason why we should less promote our own greatness and glory.

We must, therefore, make it the great business and aim of our lives to be like Christ, not in a loose or general way, but with great exactness—always looking to His spirit, His ends and designs, His ways and conversations in the world, His model and rule for our life.

Again our Savior said, "Learn of me, for I am meek and lowly of heart."[1] This is to be considered as more than good advice, but as a positive command. If we are to learn meekness and lowliness of Christ, we must do it in His way. And we must not do it in a loose or

---

1. Matthew 11:29

general sense, but in the truth and reality that characterized Christ.

There must be something very extraordinary in these dispositions of the heart. Only here does our Lord expressly say, "Learn of me." When He says this, He does not say, "I am just and equitable, or kind or holy," but "I am meek and lowly of heart," as if He would teach us that these are the tempers which most of all distinguish His spirit, and which He most of all requires His followers to learn of Him.

Was He more lowly than He need to have been? Did He practice any greater degrees of humility than were necessary? This can no more be said than that He can be charged with folly. Our great mistake would be not to follow in His steps.

Again, was our Savior's lowliness, which showed itself in an utter disregard for the pomp of life, a false lowliness that mistook its proper objects and showed itself in things not necessary? Did He abstain from dignities and splendor and deny Himself enjoyments which He might with the same lowliness of heart have taken pleasure in? If our Savior was justified as being truly and wisely humble, we condemn ourselves if we think of any other humility than such as He practiced.

If one whose life was full of bitterness and wrath and evil speaking should pretend that in his heart he loved his neighbor as himself, he would belittle his profession. To pretend to any disposition contrary to our outward actions is a similar absurdity. For a man to say he is lowly in heart while he is seeking the shows and follies of life is as absurd as for a man to say he is of a meek and forgiving spirit while he is seeking and revenging quarrels.

As there is but one way of being charitable as our Savior was, so there is but one way to be lowly in heart as He was—and that is by living in a disregard of all vain and worldly distinctions as He lived. Let us not deceive ourselves. Let us not fancy we are truly humble while living in all the pride and splendor of life. Let us not imagine we have any power to render ourselves humble and lowly any other way than by a humble and lowly course of life. Christ is our pattern and example. He did not pretend to impossibilities—to reconcile the pride of life with the lowliness of religion—but renounced the one that He might be a true example of the other.

We see the height of our calling—that we are to follow the example of our Lord and Master and to go through this world with His spirit and manner. Nothing is so likely a means to fill us with His likeness as to be frequent in reading the Gospels, which contain the history of His life and conversation in the world. We must read them as we do when we pray, not to know merely what they contain, but to fill our hearts with their spirit.

As no one prays well but he who is daily and constant in prayer, so no one can read the Scriptures to sufficient advantage but he who is daily and constant in reading them. By thus conversing with our Lord, by looking to His actions and manner of life, by hearing His divine sayings and heavenly instructions, His accounts of the terrors of the damned, His descriptions of the glory of the righteous, we should find our hearts disposed to hunger and thirst after righteousness. Happy are they who saw the Son of God upon the earth converting sinners and calling fallen spirits to return to God. And happy are we who have His discourses, doctrines, actions and miracles, which have converted Jews and heathen into saints and martyrs, still preserved to fill us with the same heavenly light and lead us to the same state of glory.

XXXVIII.
The Plausibility of Christian Perfection

WHOEVER HAS READ the foregoing chapters is, I trust, sufficiently instructed in the knowledge of Christian perfection. He has seen that it requires us to devote ourselves wholly to God, to make the ends and designs of religion the ends and designs of all our actions. It calls us to be born again of God, to live by the light of his Holy Spirit, to renounce the world and all worldly tempers, to practice a constant and universal self-denial, to make daily war with the corruption and disorder of our nature, to prepare ourselves for divine grace by a purity and holiness of conversation, to avoid all pleasures and cares which grieve the Holy Spirit and separate Him from us, to live in a constant state of prayer and devotion, and as the crown of all, to imitate the life and spirit of the holy Jesus.

It now only remains for me to exhort the reader to strive after this Christian perfection.

Were I to exhort anyone to study poetry or oratory, to labor to be rich, or to seek after various kinds of learning, I could produce only such reasons as touch upon the appearances of excellence and the transitory vanity of the world.

On the other hand, when anyone is exhorted to labor after Christian perfection, if he then asks what good it will do for him, the answer is that it will do him a good which eternity alone can measure, that it will deliver him from a state of vanity and misery and raise him from the poor enjoyments of an earthly life and give him at last a glorious body and carry him in spite of death and the grave to live with God, the angels, and all heavenly beings in infinite happiness through all eternity.

If, therefore, we could but make men so reasonable as to make the shortest inquiry into the nature of things, we should have no occasion to prod them to strive after Christian perfection. One single thought upon the eternal happiness it leads to is sufficient to make all people desire to be saints.

This shows us how inexcusable it is for those who are devoted to the things of this life. It is not that they lack deep reflections, but it is that they reject the first principles of common sense. If they were truly reasonable, they would seek after eternal happiness.

Here, therefore, I place my first argument for Christian perfection: labor after it because there is nothing else the reason of man can exhort you to. The whole world has nothing else to offer you in its stead. Choose what other way you will, and you choose nothing but vanity and misery, for all the different ways of the world are only different ways of deluding yourself. If you will make yourself more happy than those who pursue their own destruction, you must pursue that happiness and study that wisdom which leads to God. Every other pursuit, however polite or plausible in the opinions of the world, has a folly and stupidity in it.

For awhile, shut your eyes and think of the most ridiculous creature you can imagine. Now, you are that ridiculous creature if you push God aside and fail to strive after Christian perfection. Everyone has wisdom enough to see what variety of fools and madmen there are in the world. Perhaps we can do no better than to find out the true reason of the folly and madness.

If you can be content to be the poorest, vainest, most miserable creature upon earth, you may neglect Christian perfection. But if you see anything in human life that you abhor or despise, if there is any person who lives in a way in which you would fear to live, you must turn your heart to God and labor after Christian perfection, for there is nothing in nature that can set you more above the vainest, poorest, most miserable of human creatures. You are everything that you can abhor or despise, everything you can fear; you are full of every folly that your mind can imagine unless you are devoted to God.

XXXIX.
The Utter Necessity of Perfection

A SECOND ARGUMENT for Christian perfection arises from its utter necessity. I have been showing that Christian perfection consists in the right performance of our necessary duties, that it implies such holy tempers as constitute that common piety which is necessary to salvation and, consequently, equally necessary to be attained by all people. But besides this, we are to consider that God only knows what abatements of holiness He will accept; therefore we can have no security of our salvation but by doing our utmost to deserve it.

There are different degrees of holiness which it may please God to reward, but we cannot state these different degrees ourselves. We must all labor to be as eminent as we can, and then our different improvements must be left to God. We have nothing to rely on but the sincerity of our endeavors and God's mercy. Our endeavors may well be thought to want sincerity unless they are directed towards the utmost perfection. As soon as we stop at any degree of goodness, we put an end to our goodness, which is only valuable by our adding to it all that we can.

Our highest improvement is a state of great imperfection, but it will be accepted by God because it is our utmost effort. But any other state of life, where we are not doing all we can to purify and perfect our souls, is a state that can give us no comfort or satisfaction, because so far as we are wanting in any ways of piety that are in our power, so far we are defective in practical holiness that God expects. No one can have any assurance that he pleases God or puts himself within the terms of Christian salvation but he who serves God with his whole heart and with the utmost of his strength.

Though the Christian religion is a covenant of mercy for the pardon and salvation of frail imperfect creatures, yet we cannot say that we are within the conditions of that mercy until we do all we can in our frail and imperfect state. Although we are not called to a sinless state of perfection, and though our imperfections will not prevent divine mercy, yet it cannot be proved that God has any terms of favor for those who do not strive to be as perfect as they can be.

Different attainments of piety will doubtless carry different persons to heaven, yet none of us can have any confidence that we are going there but by arriving at all the change of nature which is in our power. It is as necessary, therefore, to labor after perfection as to labor after our salvation, because we can have no satisfaction that a failure in one will not deprive us of the other. When you are exhorted to Christian perfection, you must remember that you are only exhorted to secure your salvation. You must remember, also, that you have no other rule to judge of your perfection but by the sincerity and fullness of your endeavors to arrive at it.

We may judge of the measure and extent of Christian holiness by its possession of charity. This virtue is thus described, "[Charity] seeketh not her own . . . beareth all things, believeth all things, hopeth all things, endureth all things."[1] This charity, which is a part of perfection, is made by the Apostle so absolutely necessary to salvation that a failure in it is not to be supplied by any other of the most shining virtues: "Though I have all faith, so that I could remove mountains, though I bestow all my goods to feed the poor, though I give my body to be burned and have not charity, it profiteth me nothing."[2]

The Apostle expressly teaches us that this perfection in Christian charity is so necessary to salvation that even martyrdom itself is not sufficient to atone for the want of it. What is here said of charity must be understood of every other virtue; it must be practiced in the same fullness and sincerity of heart as this charity. It may also be affirmed that this charity is so holy a temper and requires so many other virtues as the foundation of it that it can only be exercised by a heart that is so far advanced in holiness as to be entirely devoted to God.

Do not imagine that it belongs only to people of a particular piety and turn of mind to labor after their perfection and that you may go to heaven with much less care. There is only one "strait gate" and one "narrow way" that leads unto life; there is no admission but for those who strive to enter into it. If you are not striving, you neglect the express condition which our Lord requires, and it is flat nonsense to think that you strive if you do not use all your strength.

The Apostle represents a Christian's striving for eternal life in this manner, "Know ye not that they which run in a race run all, but one receiveth the prize? So run that ye may obtain."[3] Accordingly, only he is on the road to salvation who is contending for it as he that is running in a race. Further, you can have no satisfaction that you are sincere in any one virtue unless you are endeavoring to be perfect in all the instances of it.

If you allow yourself any defects of charity, you have no reason to think yourself sincere in any acts of charity. If you indulge yourself in any instances of pride, you render all your acts of humility suspect, because there can be no true reason for charity but what is a good reason for all instances of charity, nor any religious motive for humility but what is a strong motive for all degrees of humility. He

---

1. I Corinthians 13:5,7   2. I Corinthians 13:2,3   3. I Corinthians 9:24

who allows himself any known defects of charity, humility, or any other virtue, cannot be supposed to practice any instances of that virtue upon true reasons of religion. If it was a right fear of God, a true desire of being like Christ, a hearty love of my fellow creatures that made me give alms, the same disposition would make me love and forgive all my enemies and deny myself all kinds of revenge and spite and evil-speaking.

Every instance of uncharitableness is the same sin against charity as the refusal of alms, for the refusal of alms is only a great sin because it shows that we have not a right fear of God nor a hearty desire to be like Christ; also we lack a true love for our fellowmen. As every allowed instance of uncharitableness shows a want of all these tempers, so it shows that every such instance is the same sin and sets us as far from God as the refusal of alms.

To forbear from spite and evil-speaking is a proper act of Christian charity, but it is such a charity as will not profit those who are not charitable in giving to those in need, because by refusing alms, they sin against as many reasons of charity as he who lives in spite and evil-speaking. On the other hand, he who allows himself to engage in evil-speaking sins against all the same reasons of charity as he who lives in refusal of alms.

Humility is much better discovered by our behavior towards our equals and superiors than towards those who are below us. It does no hurt to a proud heart to stoop to some low offices of the meanest people. Indeed, there is something in it that may gratify pride, for perhaps our own greatness is never seen to more advantage than when we stoop to those who are far below us. The lower the people are to whom we stoop, the better they show the height of our own state. Such condescensions are no contradictions to pride.

The truest trial of humility is our behavior towards our equals and those who are our superiors or inferiors but in a small degree. It is no sign of humility for a private gentleman to pay a profound reverence and great submission to a king, nor is it any sign of humility for the same person to condescend to great familiarity with a poor almsman; he may act upon the same principle in both cases. It does not hurt him to show great submission to a king because he has no thoughts of being equal to a king, and for the same reason it does not hurt him to condescend to poor people because he never imagines that they will think themselves equal to him.

From this it appears that our most splendid acts of virtue, which we think may be sufficient to atone for our other known defects, may themselves be so vain and defective as to have no merit in them. This also shows us the absolute necessity of laboring after all instances of perfection in every virtue, because if we pick and choose what parts of any virtue we will perform, we sin against all the same reasons, as if we neglected all parts of it. If we choose to give instead of forgiving, we choose something other than charity.

XL.
Perfection and Eternal Glory

ANOTHER MOTIVE to induce you to aspire after Christian perfection may be taken from the double advantage of it in this life and that which is to come.

The Apostle exhorts the Corinthians, "Wherefore, my beloved brethren, be ye steadfast, immovable, always abounding in the work of the Lord, forasmuch as ye know that our labor will not be in vain in the Lord."[1] This exhortation is founded upon solid reason, for what can be so wise and reasonable as to be always abounding in that work which will never be in vain? While we are pleased with ourselves, or pleased with the world, we are pleased with vanity, and our most prosperous labors are, as the Preacher says, "but vanity of vanities, all is vanity." But while we are striving for Christian perfection, we are laboring for eternity and building for ourselves higher stations in the joys of heaven.

"As one star differeth from another star in glory, so also is the resurrection of the dead."[2] We shall surely rise to different degrees of

---

1. I Corinthians 15:58   2. I Corinthians 15:41b-42a

glory, of joy and happiness in God according to our different advancements in purity, holiness, and good works.

No degrees of mortification and self-denial, no private prayers, no secret mournings, no instances of charity, no labors of love will ever be forgotten, but all will be treasured up to our everlasting comfort and refreshment. For though the rewards of the other life are free gifts of God, yet since He has assured us that every man shall be rewarded according to his works, it is certain that our rewards will be as different as our works have been.

Stand still awhile and ask yourself whether you really believe it to be true that the more perfect we make ourselves here the more happy we shall be hereafter. If you do not believe this to be strictly true, you know nothing of God or true religion. And if you believe it to be true, is it possible to be awake and not aspire after Christian perfection?

If you would now devote yourself to perfection, perhaps you must part with some friends, you must lay aside some designs, you must refrain from some pleasures, you must alter your life—nay, perhaps you must even expose yourself to the hatred of some and to the scorn and derision of worldly men. But had you not better suffer all this than to die less perfect and less prepared for mansions of eternal glory?

Fancy yourself living in all the ease and pleasure that the world can give you, esteemed by your friends, undisturbed by your enemies, and gratifying all your natural desires. If you could stand still in such a state, it may hold some merit. But, alas, every day that is added to such a life is the same thing as a day taken from it and shows that so much happiness is gone from you. For be as happy as you will, you must see it all sinking away from you; you must feel yourself declining and see that your time shortens apace. You must both dread and desire old age, for as death approaches, you must know that you will die in the painful sorrows of deep repentance or in gloomy despair of wishing for the mountains to fall on you and the seas to cover you. Is this a happiness to be chosen? Is it worth your while to separate yourself from God, to lose your share in the realms of light?

You may be so blind and foolish as not to think of these things, but it is impossible to think of them seriously without laboring after Christian perfection. It may be you are too young, too happy, or too busy to be affected by these reflections, but be warned, all will be over before you are aware. Your day will be quickly spent and leave you to such a night as that which surprised the foolish virgins. And at midnight "there was a great cry made, behold the bridegroom cometh; go ye out to meet him."[3]

The last hour will soon be with you when you will have nothing to look for but your reward in another life, when you will stand with nothing before you but eternity, and you must begin to be something that will be your state forever. I can no more reach heaven with my hands than I can describe the emotions you will then have. You will then feel motions of heart never before experienced. All your thoughts and reflections will pierce your soul in a manner unknown before. You will feel the immortality of your nature by the depth and piercing vigor of your thoughts. You will then know what it means to die—that dying thoughts are as new and amazing as that state which follows them.

Let me therefore, exhort you to come prepared to this time of trial, to look out for comfort while the day is before you, to treasure up such a fund of good and pious works as may make you able to bear that which cannot be borne without them. Could I in any way make you apprehend how dying men want a pious life, how they lament time lost, health and strength squandered away in folly, how they look to eternity, and what they think of the rewards of another life, you would soon find yourself one of those who desires to live in the highest state of piety and perfection. You could then grow old in peace and die in full hope of eternal glory.

Consider again, that besides the rewards of the other life, laboring after Christian perfection by devoting yourself wholly to God has a great reward even in this life as it makes religion doubly pleasant to you. When you are divided between God and the world, you have neither the pleasures of religion nor the pleasures of the world, but are always in the uneasiness of a divided heart. You dare

3. Matthew 25:6

not wholly neglect religion, but you take no more than is just sufficient to keep you from being a terror to yourself; you are as loath to be very good as you are fearful to be very bad. This is a state of half-piety.

Let me exhort you to a solid state of piety, that by entering deep into religion you may enter deep into its comforts, that by serving God with all your heart you may have the peace and pleasure of a heart that is a unity. When your conscience once bears you witness that you are "steadfast, immovable, always abounding in the work of the Lord,"[4] you will find that your reward has already begun and that you could not be less devout or charitable without lessening the most substantial pleasure in your life. To be content with any lower attainments of piety is to rob yourself of a present happiness that nothing else can give.

You would perhaps devote yourself to perfection but for some little difficulty that lies in your way, or if you were in a more convenient state for the practice of piety. But this is nonsense, because perfection consists of conquering difficulties. You could not be perfect, as the present state of trial requires, had you not those difficulties and inconveniences to struggle with. The things you would have removed are laid in your way that you may make them steps to perfection and glory.

If all your friends and acquaintances were devout and heavenly-minded, it would be less perfection in you to be like them. But if you are humble among those who delight in pride, heavenly-minded among the worldly, sober among the intemperate, and devout among the irreligious, then are you truly devoted to God. You can have no difficulty but what the world lays in your way. Perfection is never to be had but by parting with the world. To wait to be perfect until it suits with your conditions in the world is like waiting to be charitable until there are no objects of charity, or to be courageous until some time when there is nothing left to try your courage.

The foolish virgins who had provided no oil for their lamps and who were shut out of the marriage feast were foolish only so far as they trusted to the assistance of those who were wise. But you are

---

4. I Corinthians 15:58

more foolish than they, for you trust to be saved by the folly of others when you imagine yourself safe in negligence, vanity, and irregularity of the world. You take confidence in the broad way because it is broad and you are content with yourself because you seem to be one of the "many" though God Himself has told you that "narrow is the way that leadeth unto life, and few there be that find it."[5]

One word more. Think what a happiness it is that you have it in your power to secure a share in the glories of heaven and to make yourself one of those blessed beings that live with God forever. Reflect upon the glories of bright angels who shine about the throne of heaven. Think upon the fullness of joy which is the state of Christ at the right hand of God and remember it is this same state of glory and joy that lies open for you. It may be you are less in worldly distinctions than many others, but as to your relation to God, you have no superior upon earth.

Let your condition be what it will, let your life be ever so mean, you may make the end of it the beginning of eternal glory.

Reflect often upon this that you may be filled with a wise ambition for all that glory to which God in Christ has called you. It is impossible to understand anything of this without feeling your heart affected by a strong desire for it. The hopes and expectations of so much greatness and glory must awaken you to earnest desires and longings after it.

There are many things in this life after which it would be vain for you to aspire, but the happiness of the next, which is the sum of all happiness, is secure and safe against all accidents. Here no chances or misfortunes can prevent your success; neither the treachery of friends nor the malice of enemies can disappoint you. It is only your own false heart that can rob you of this happiness. Be but your own true friend, and then you have nothing to fear. Sincerely labor in the Lord, and then neither height nor depth, neither life nor death, neither men nor devils can make you labor in vain.

---

5. Matthew 7:14

Other Books by William Law

Wholly for God
The Power of the Spirit
Freedom from a Self-Centered Life